INCURABLY MAD !

by Sergio Aragones

Edited by Albert B. Feldstein

WARNER BOOKS

A Warner Communications Company

WARNER BOOKS EDITION

Copyright © 1977 by Sergio Aragones
and E.C. Publications, Inc.

This Warner Books Edition is published by
arrangement with E.C. Publications, Inc.

Warner Books, Inc., 75 Rockefeller Plaza, New York, N.Y. 10019

 A Warner Communications Company

Printed in the United States of America

First Printing: March, 1977

Reissued: September, 1985

10   9

To Nick Meglin

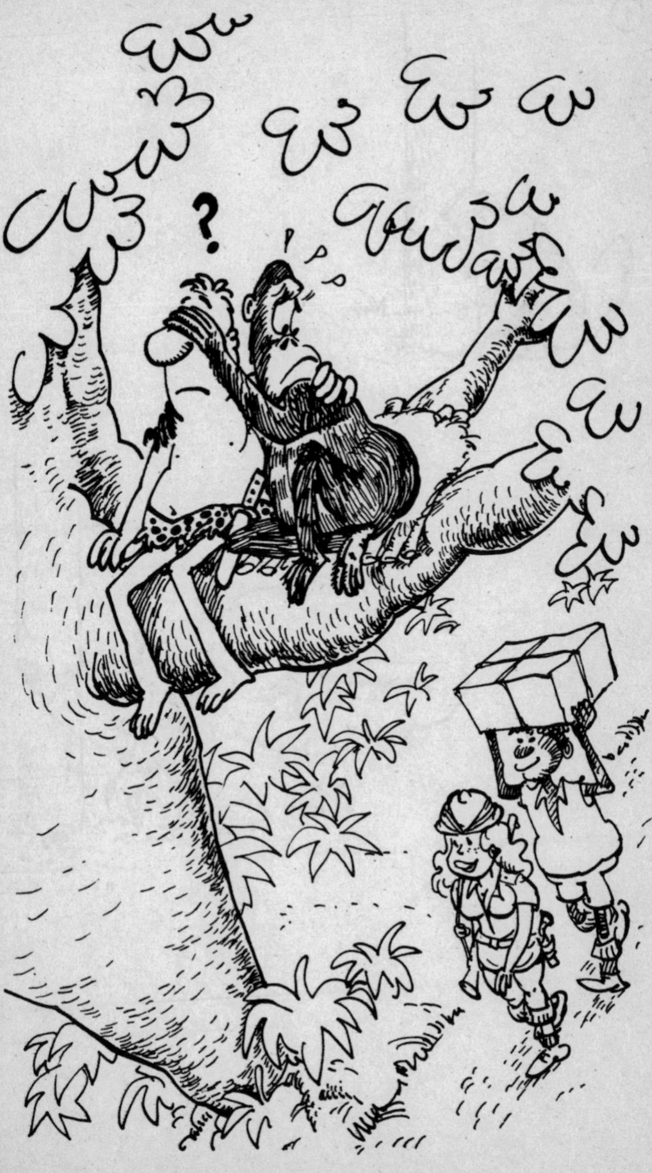

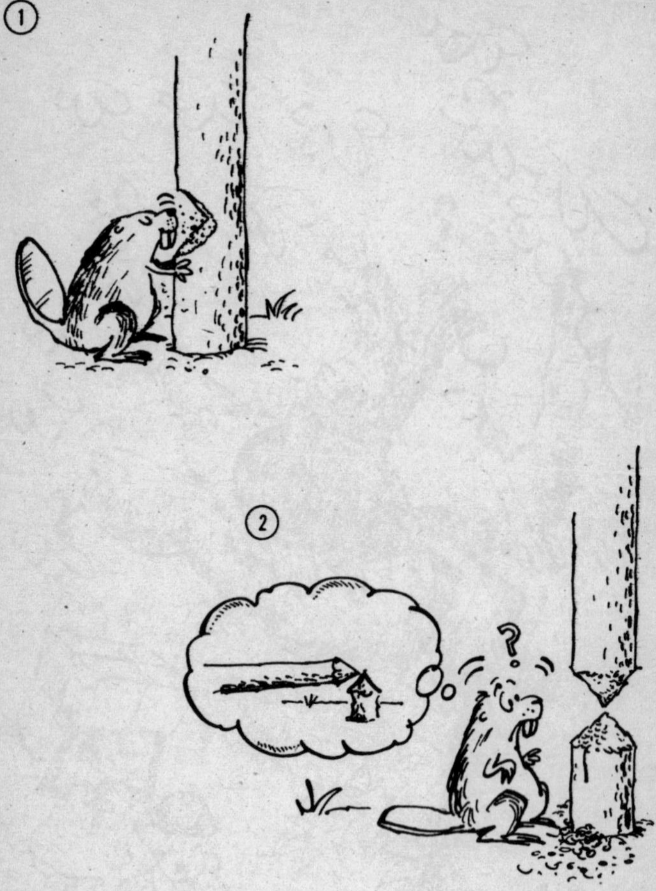
1
2
?

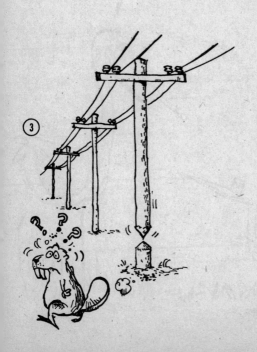

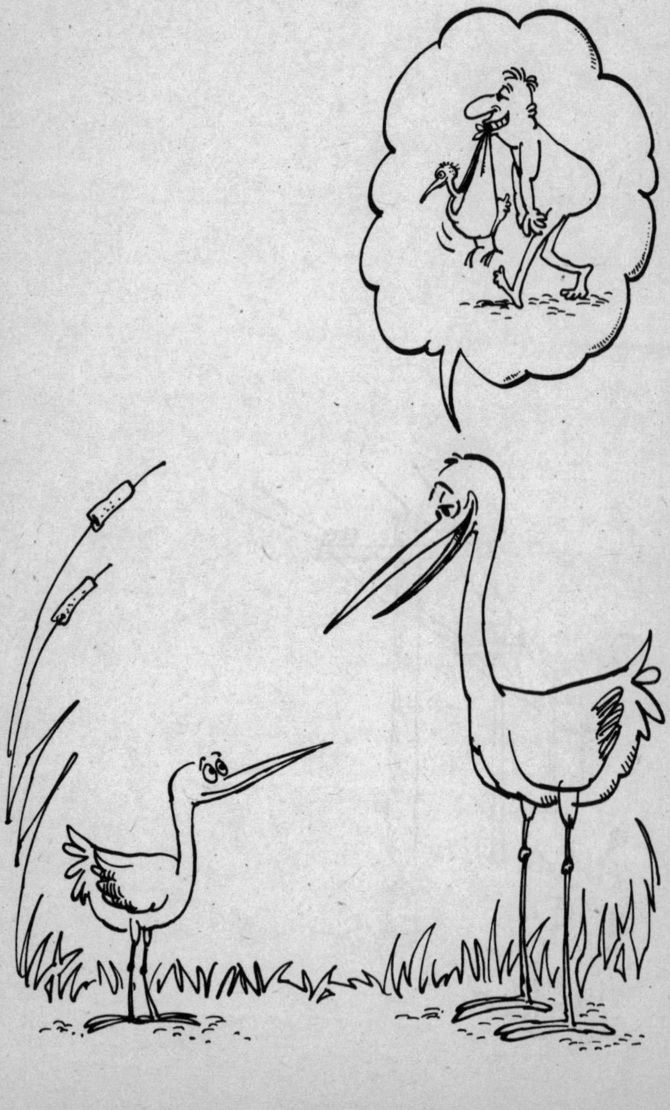

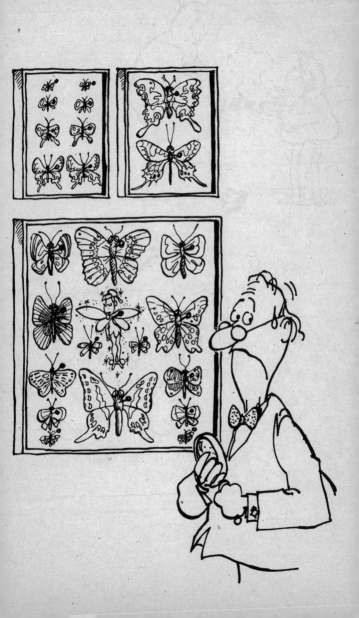

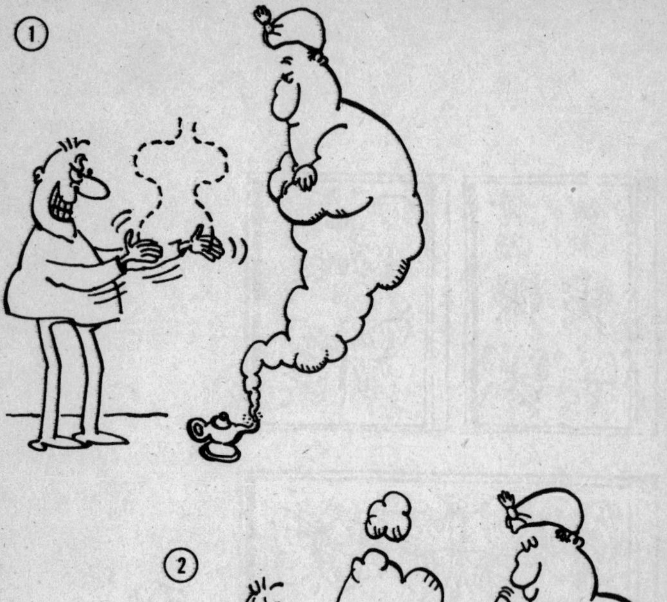
1
2
POOF!

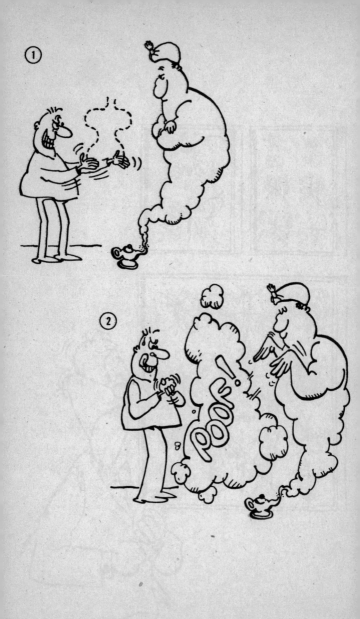

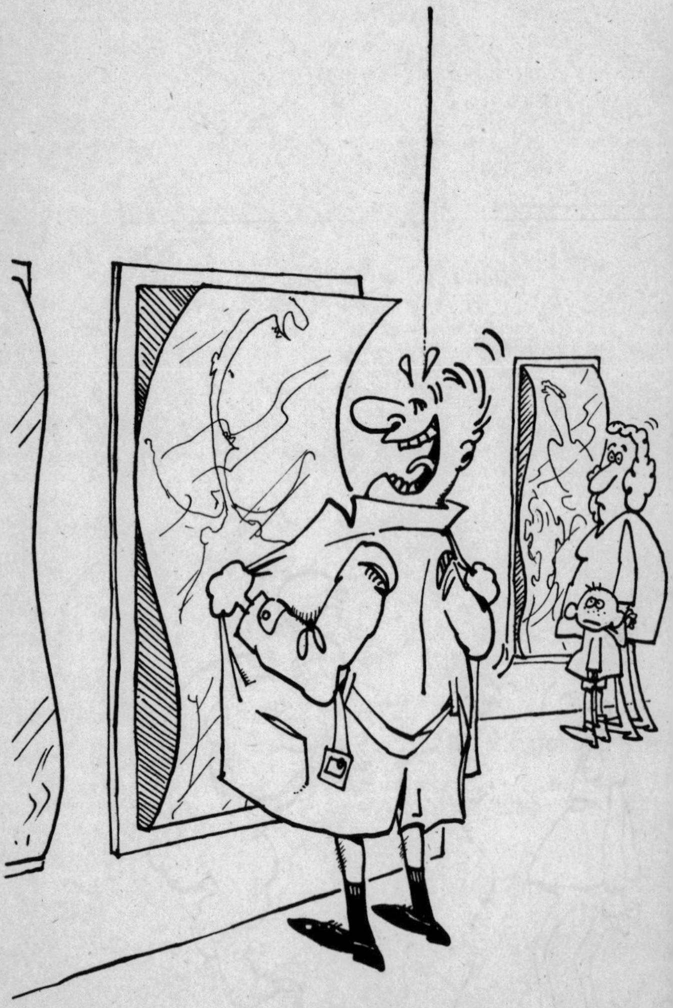

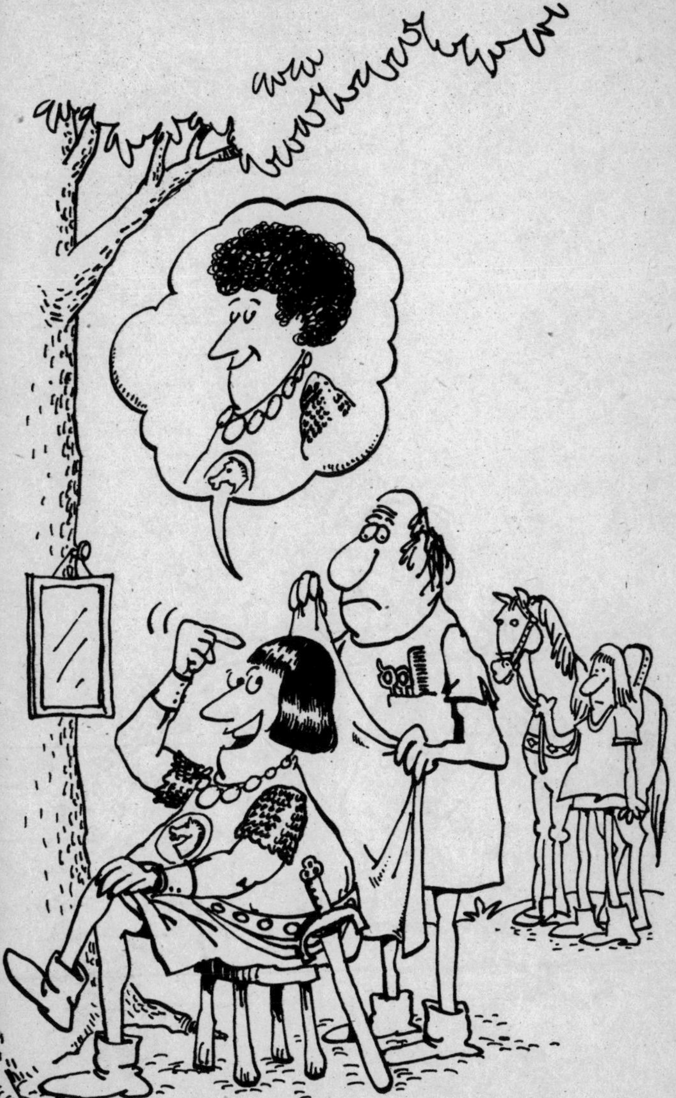

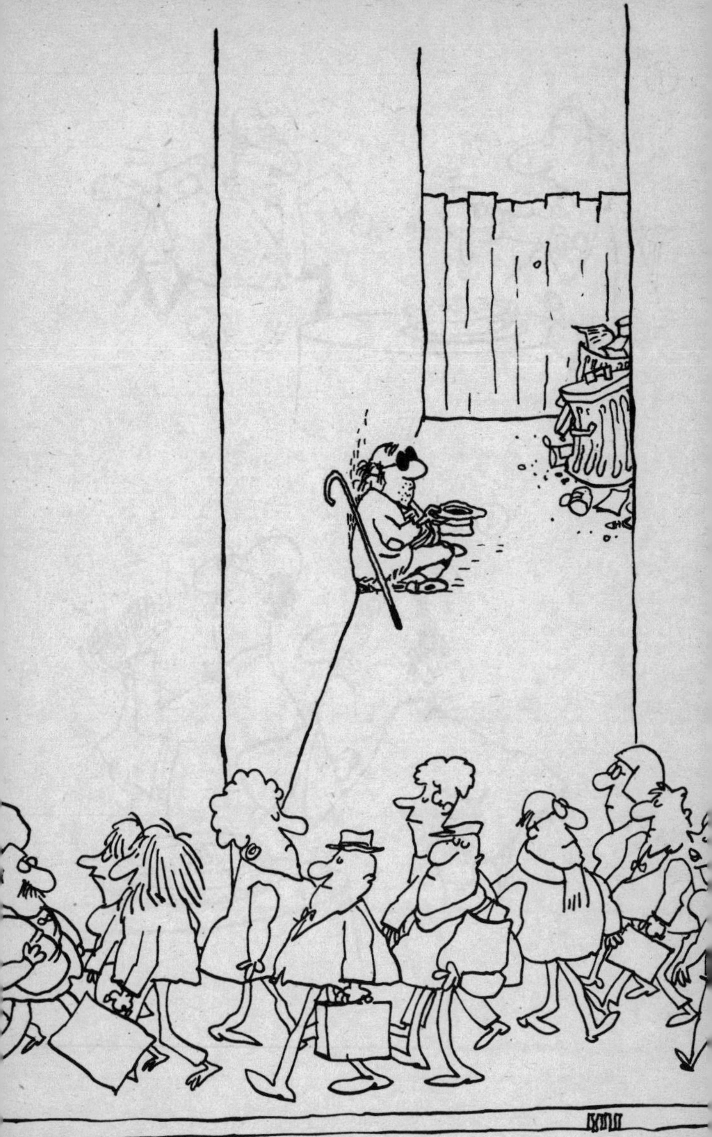

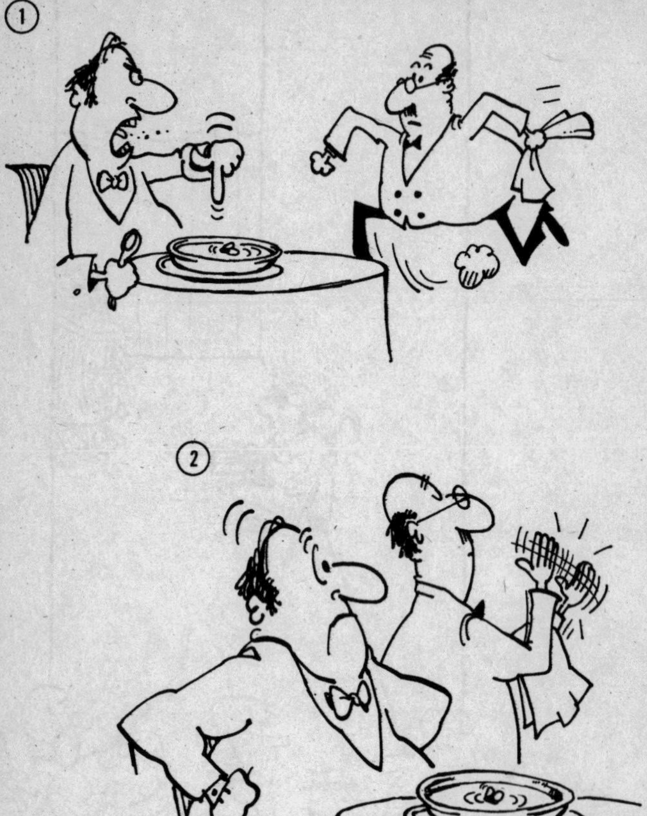
1
2

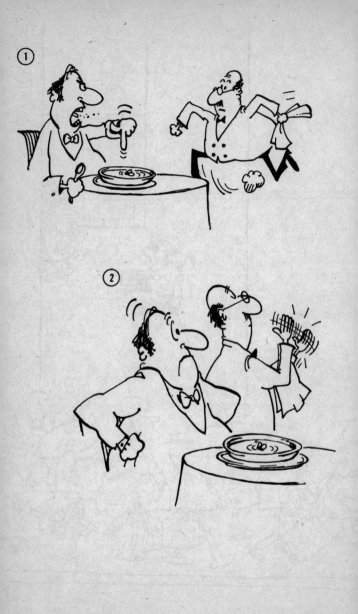

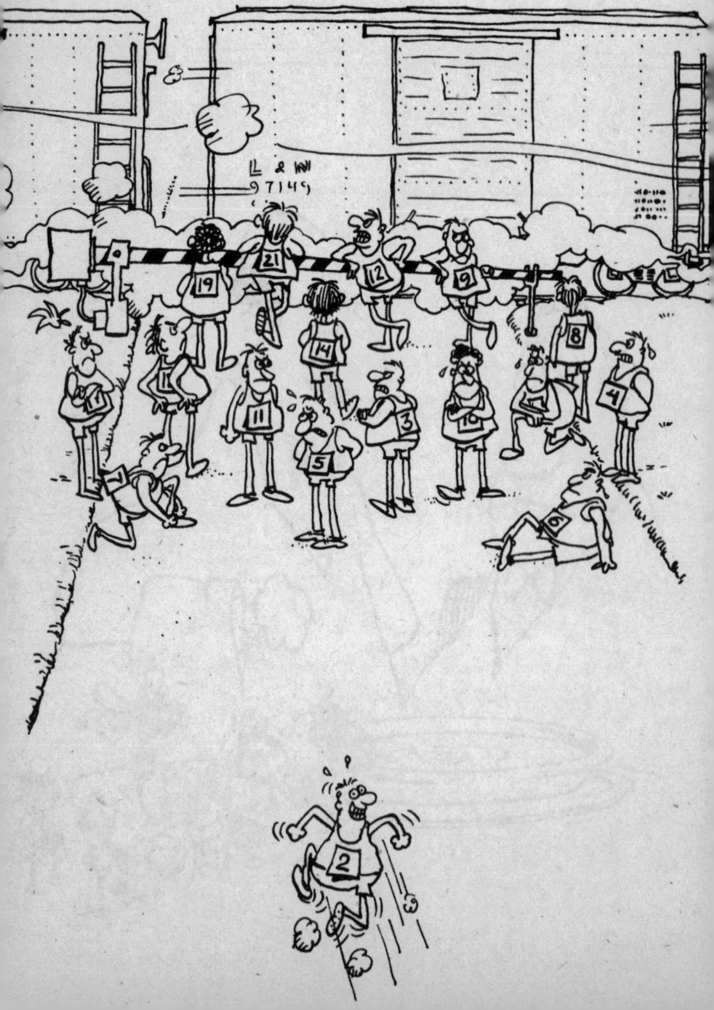

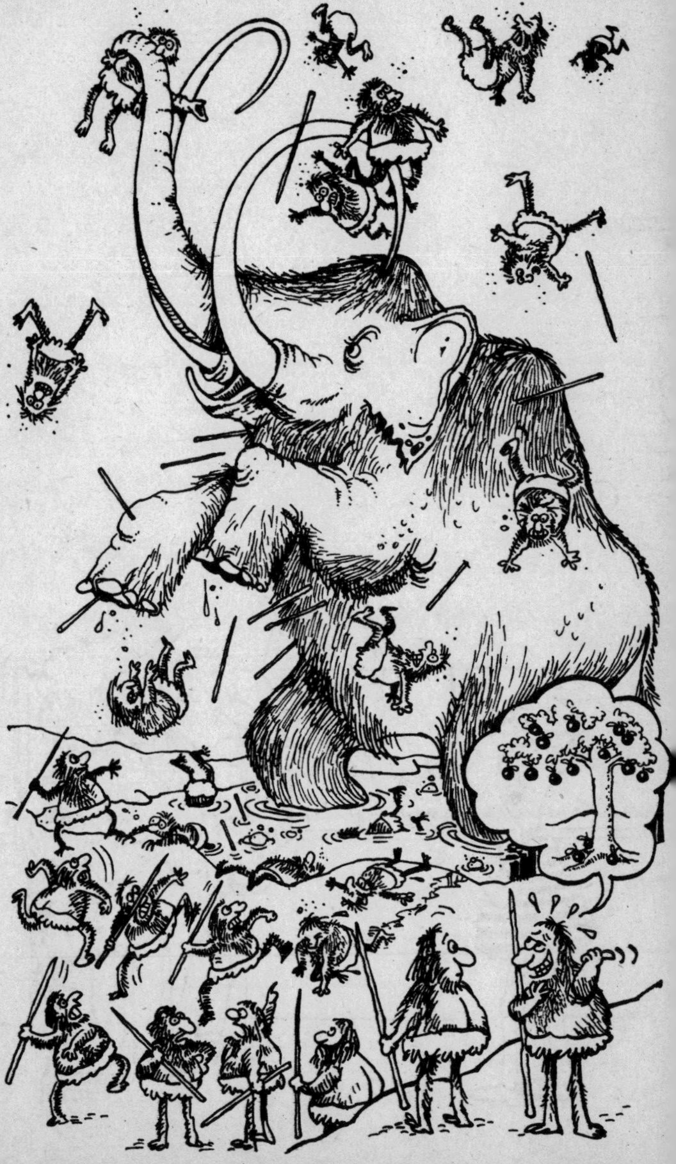

①

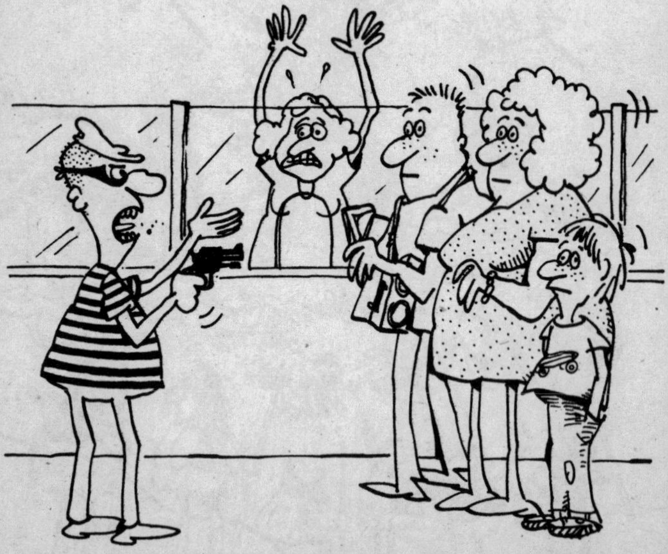

(2)

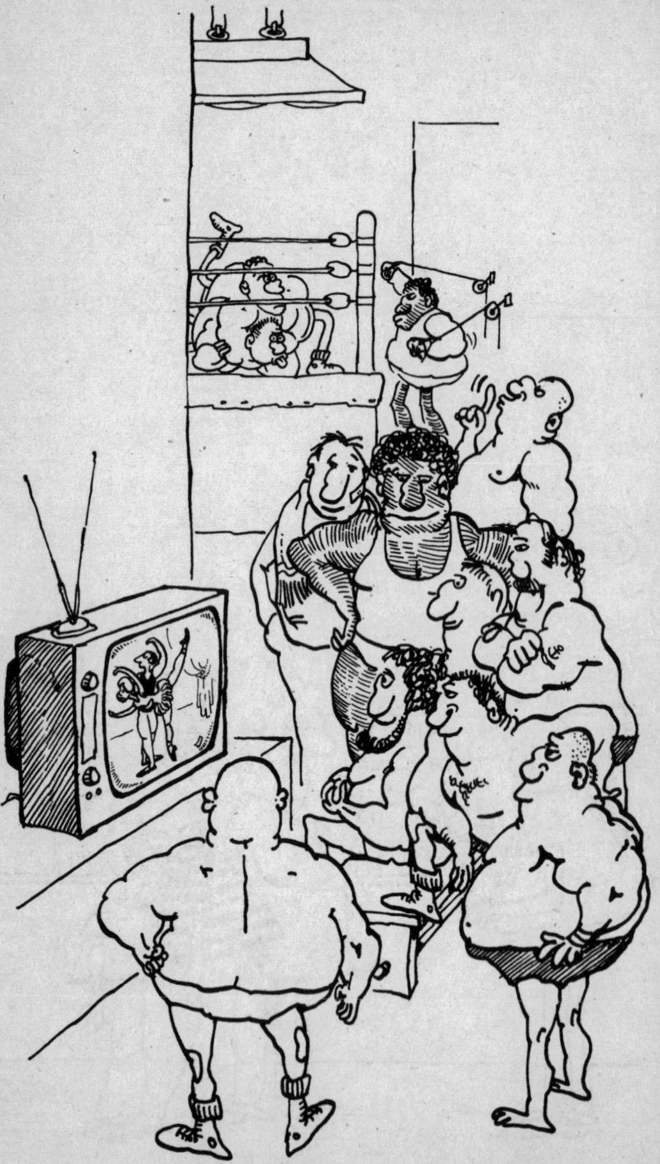

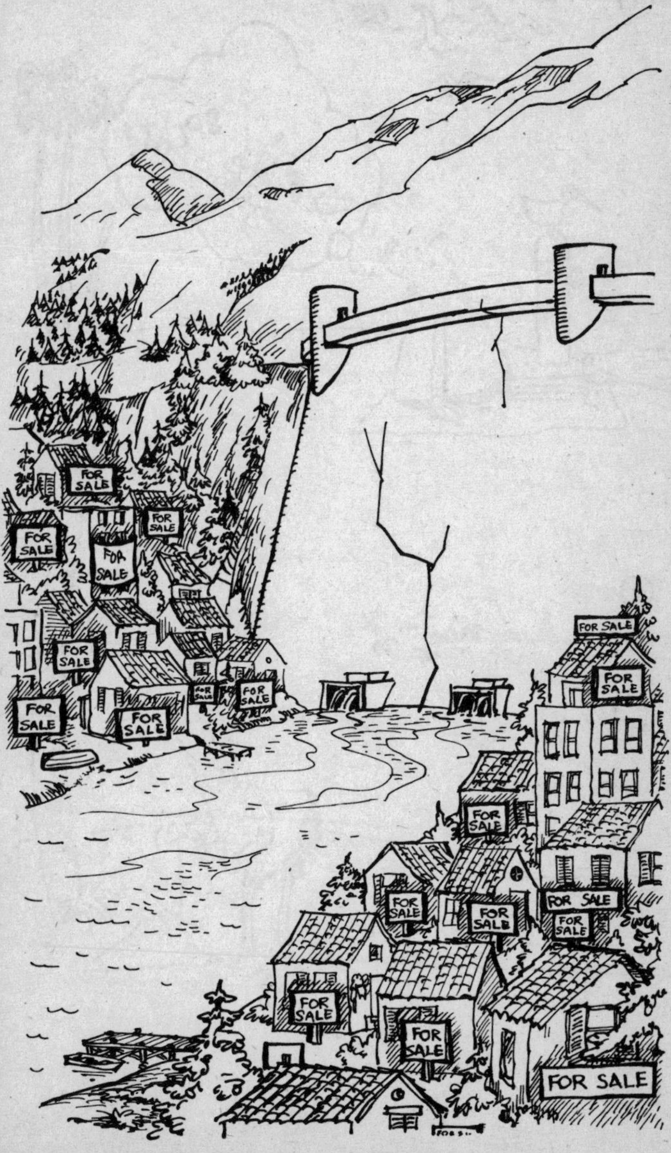
FOR SALE
FOR SALE
FOR SALE
FOR SALE
FOR SALE
FOR SALE
FOR SALE
FOR SALE
FOR SALE
FOR SALE
FOR SALE
FOR SALE
FOR SALE
FOR SALE
FOR SALE
FOR SALE
FOR SALE
FOR SALE
FOR SALE

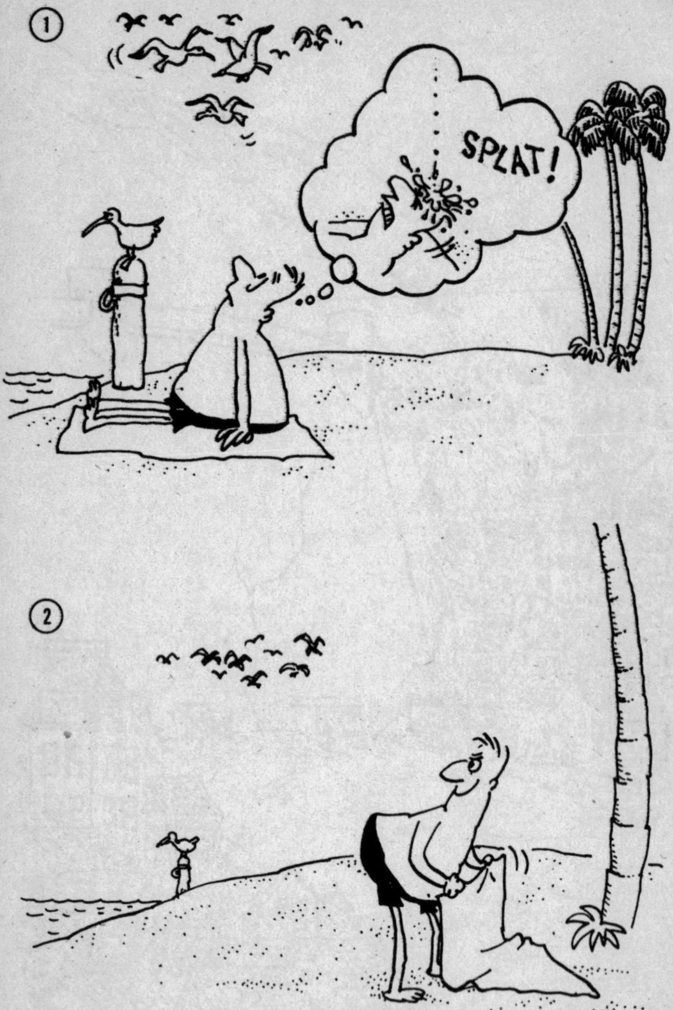
1
SPLAT!
2

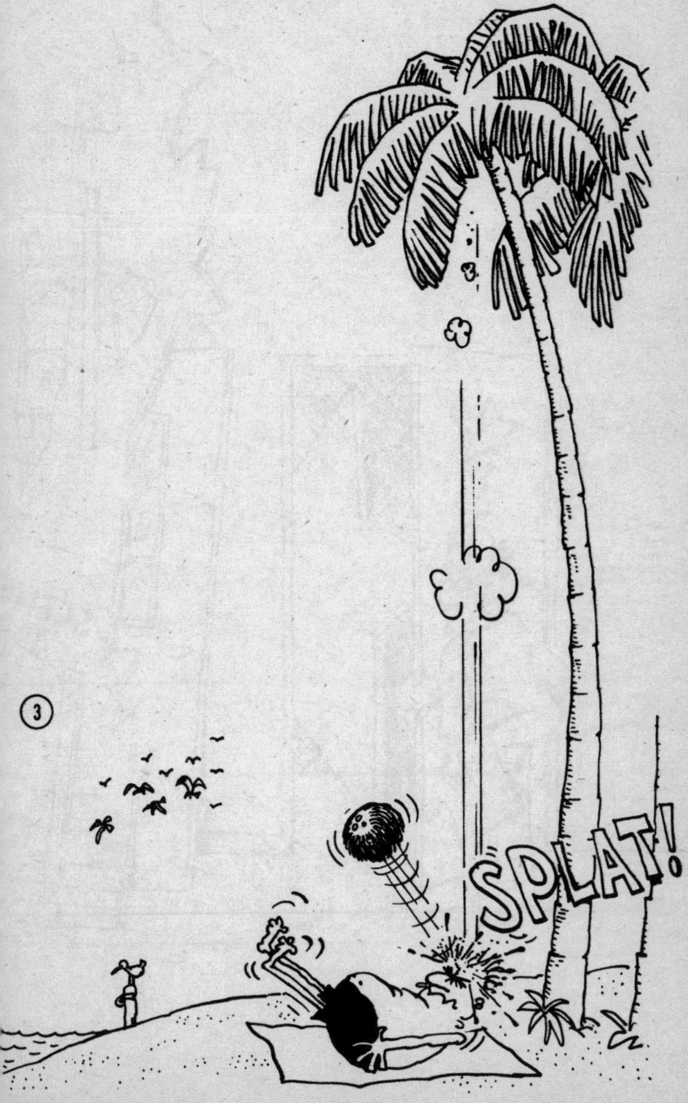
③
SPLAT!

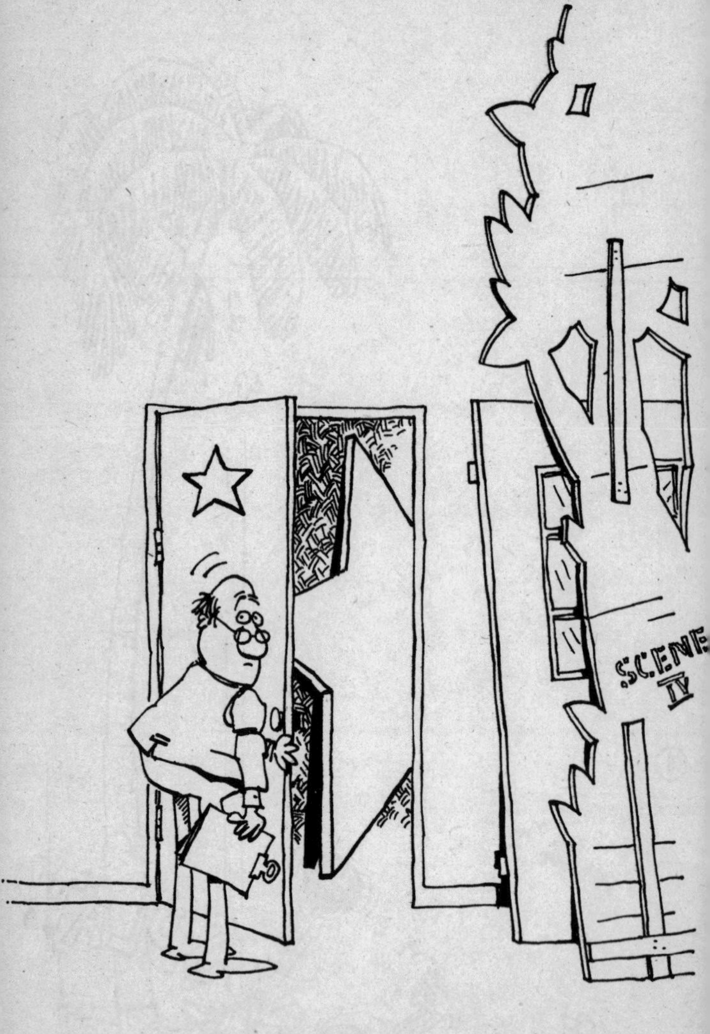
SCENE
IV

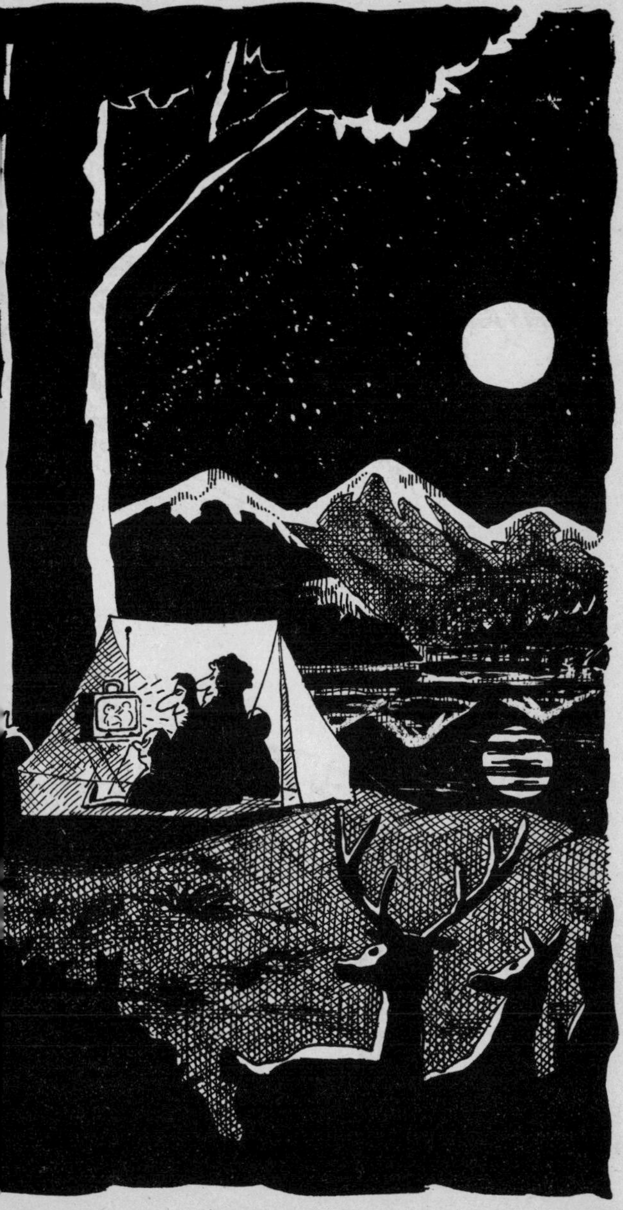

1

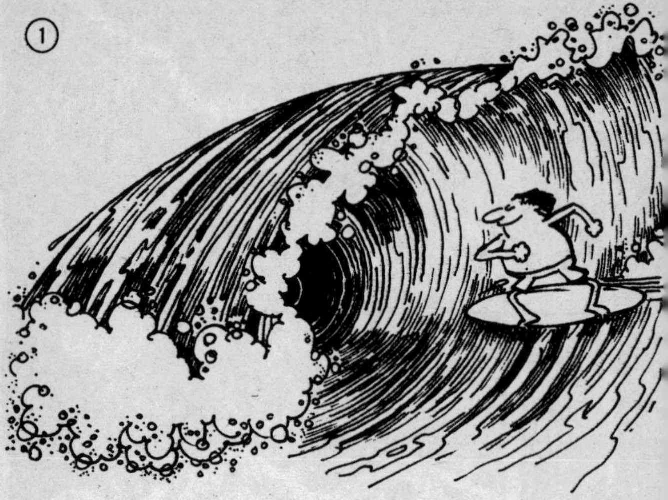

2

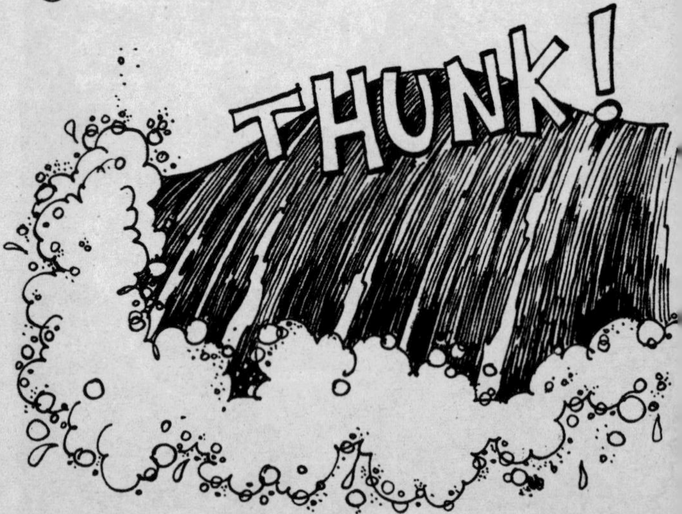
THUNK!

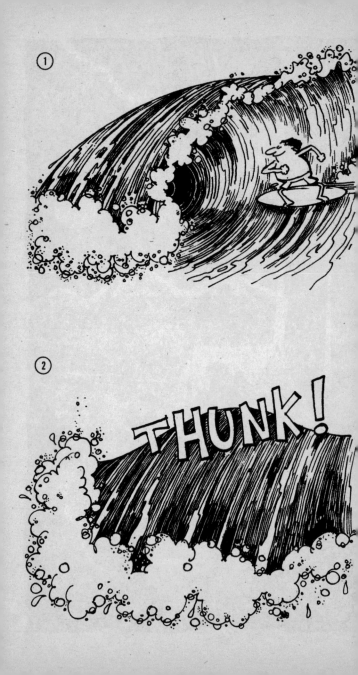

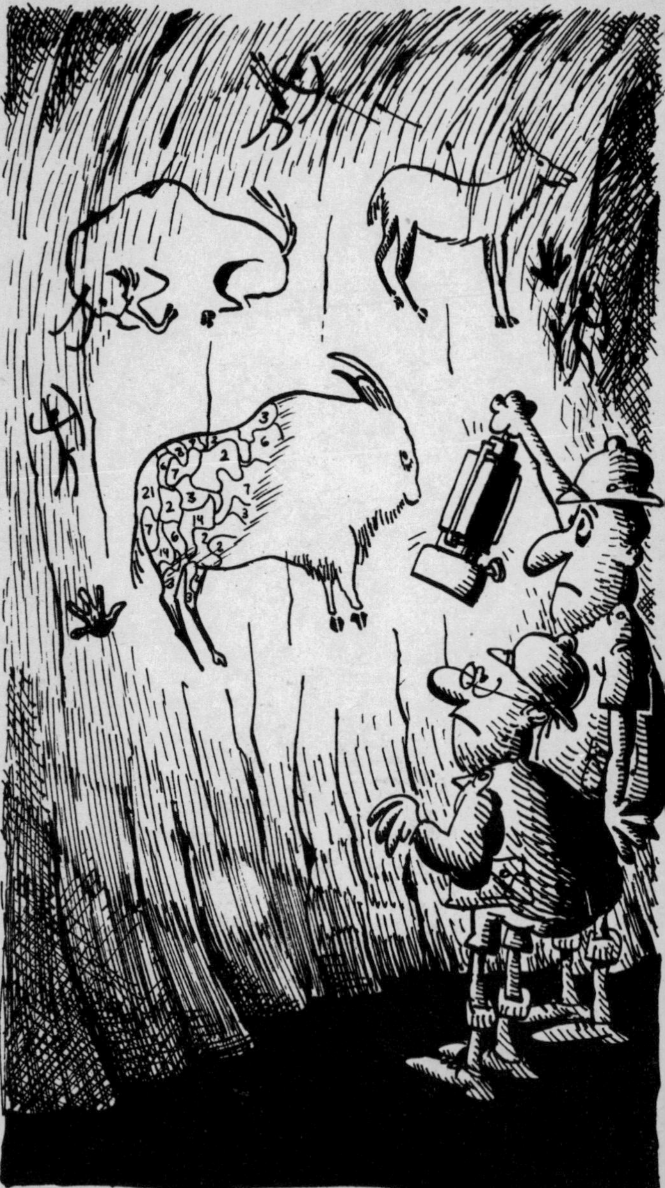

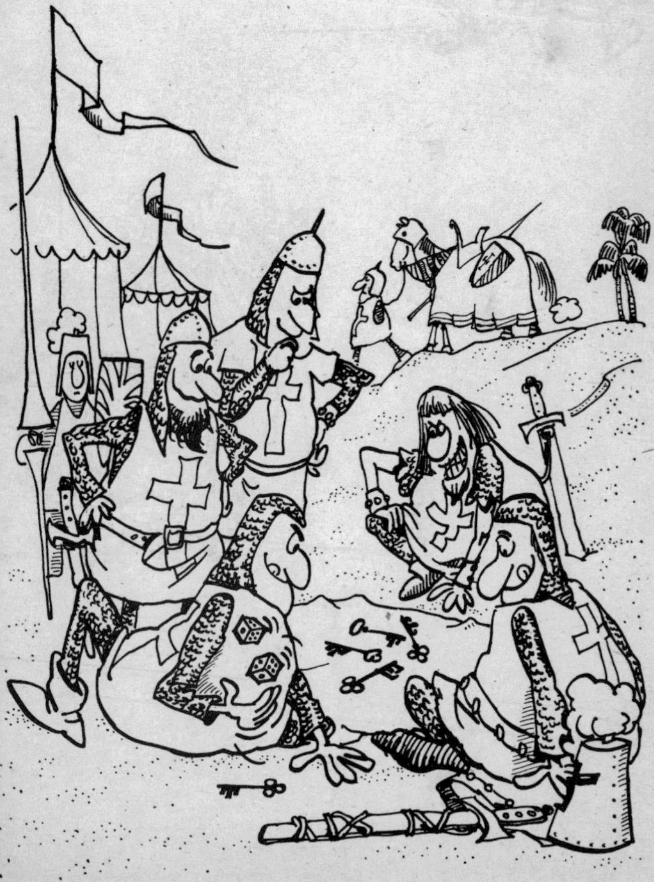

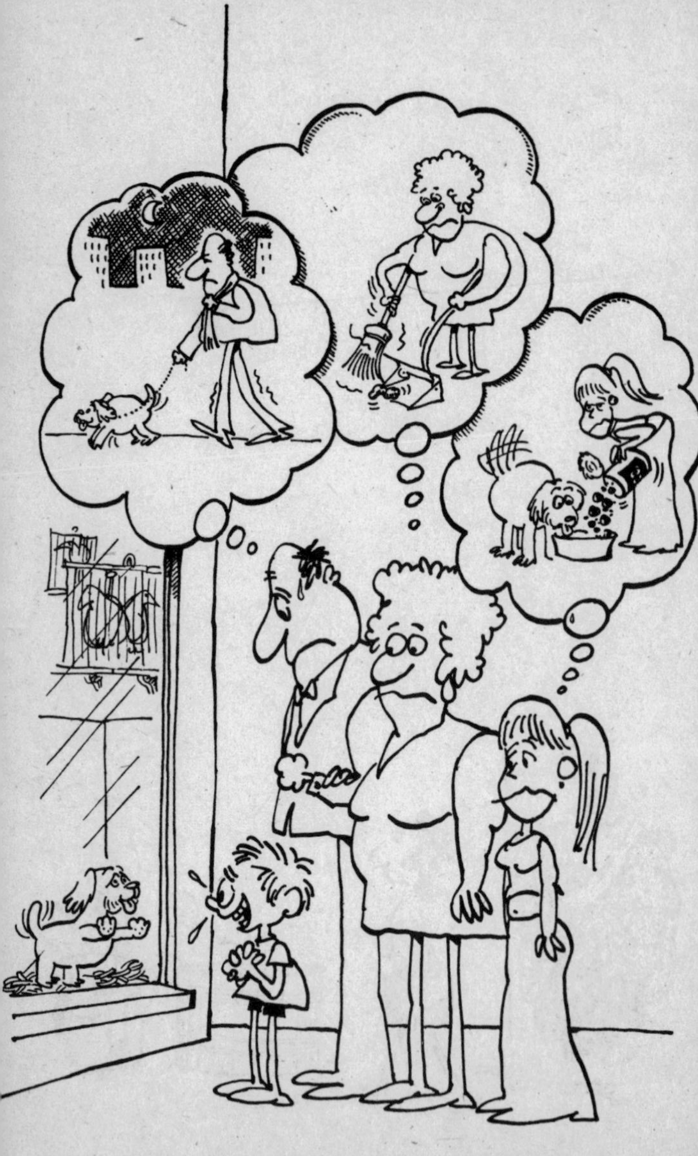

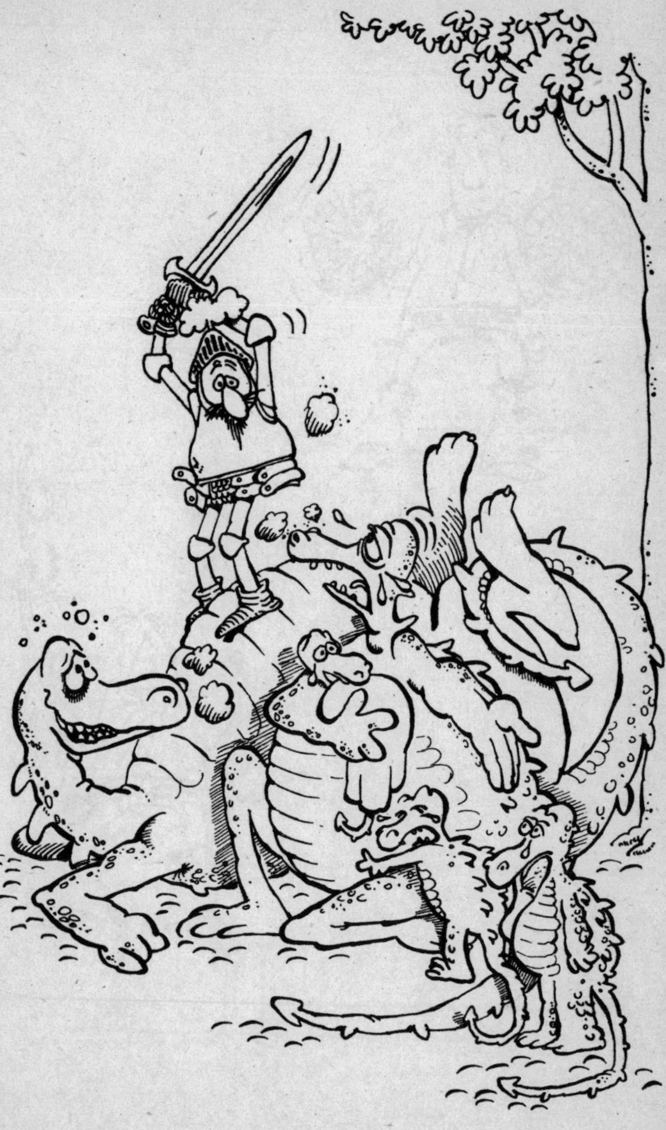

1

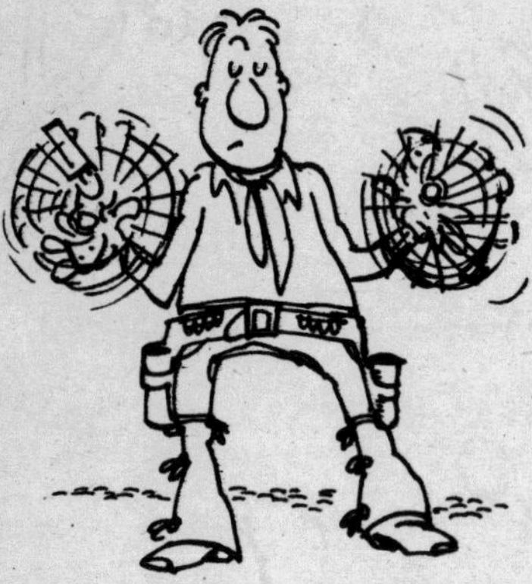

2

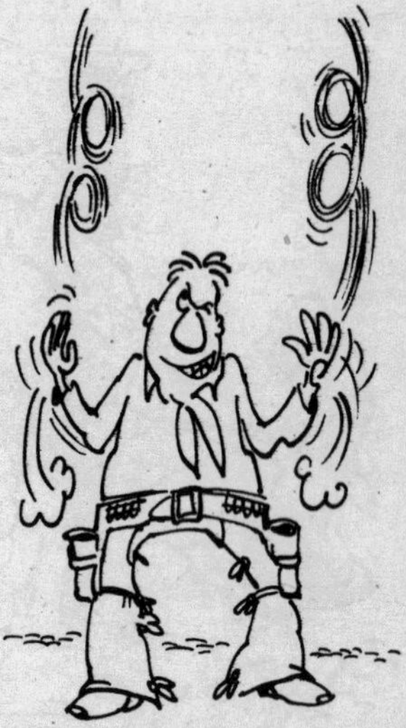

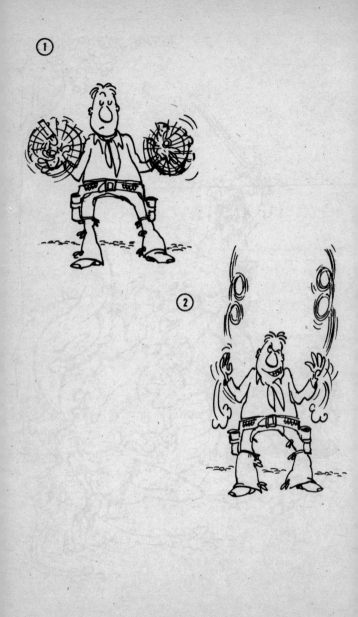

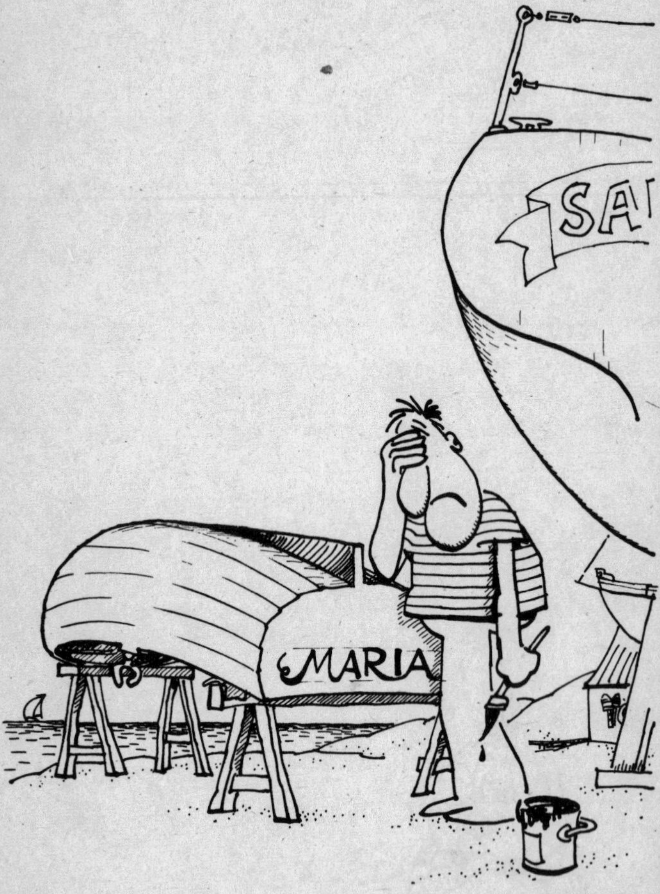
SA
MARIA

1

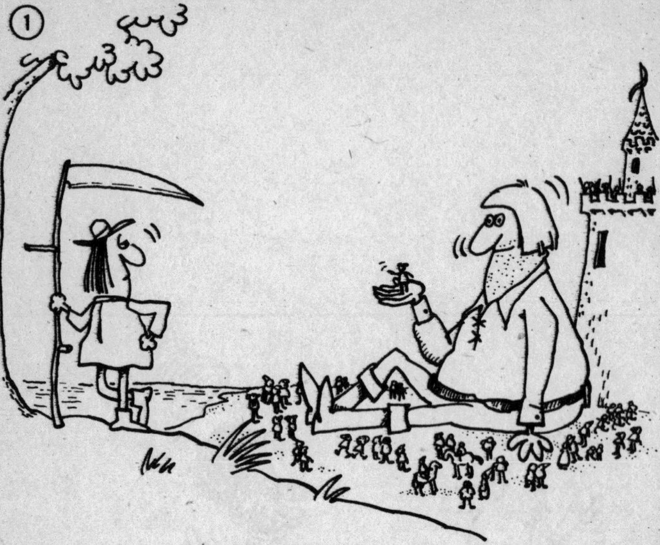

2

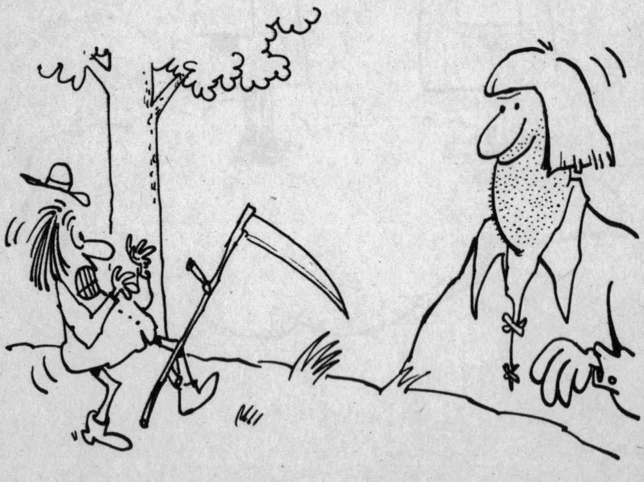

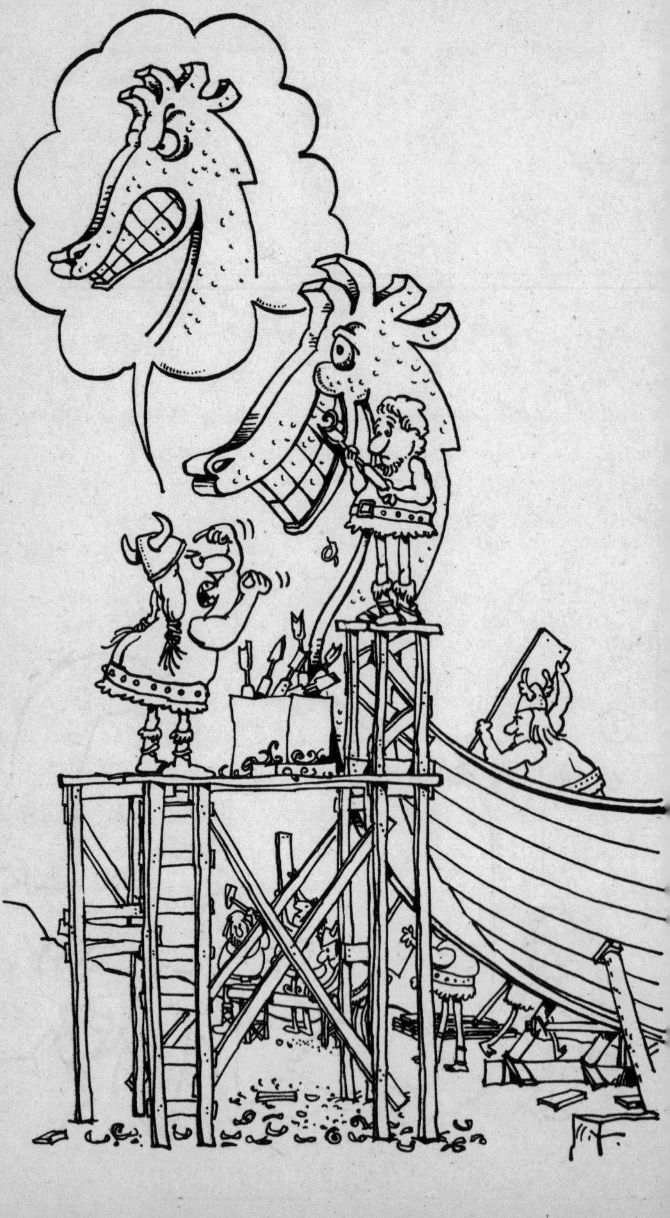

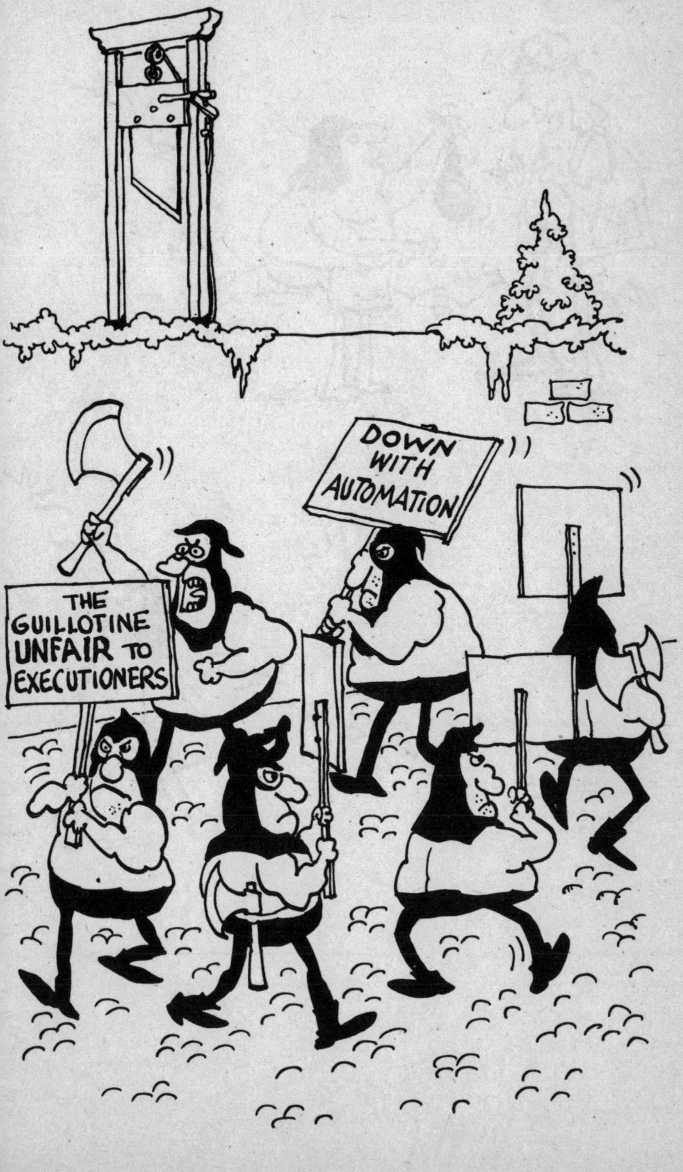
DOWN
WITH
AUTOMATION
THE
GUILLOTINE
UNFAIR TO
EXECUTIONERS

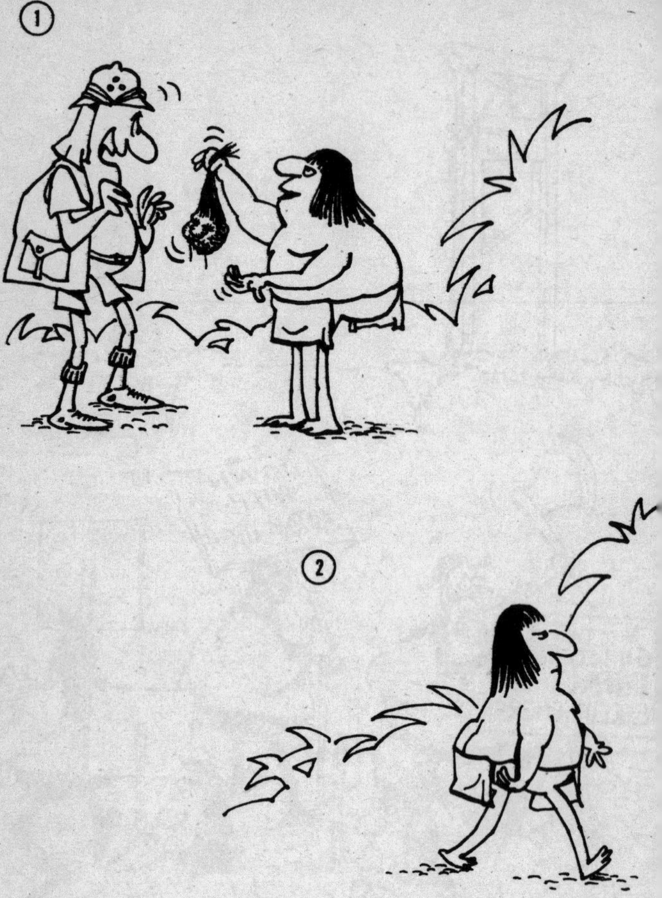
1
2

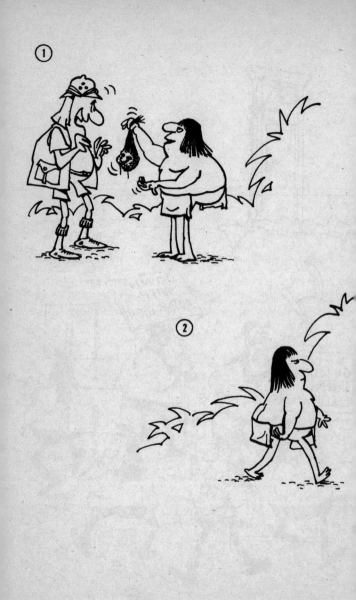

3

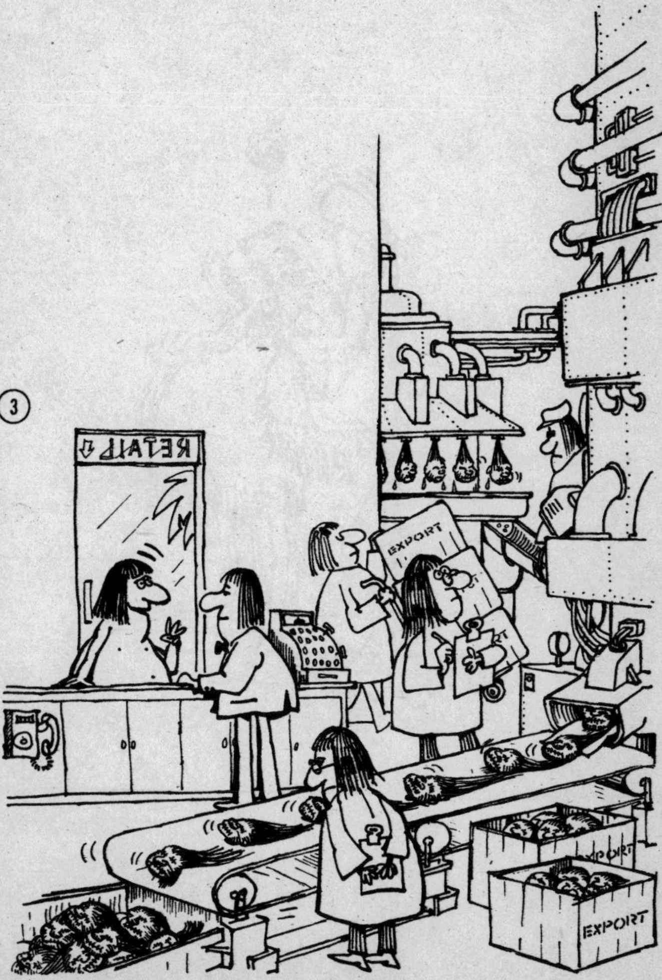

RETAIL
EXPORT
EXPORT
EXPORT

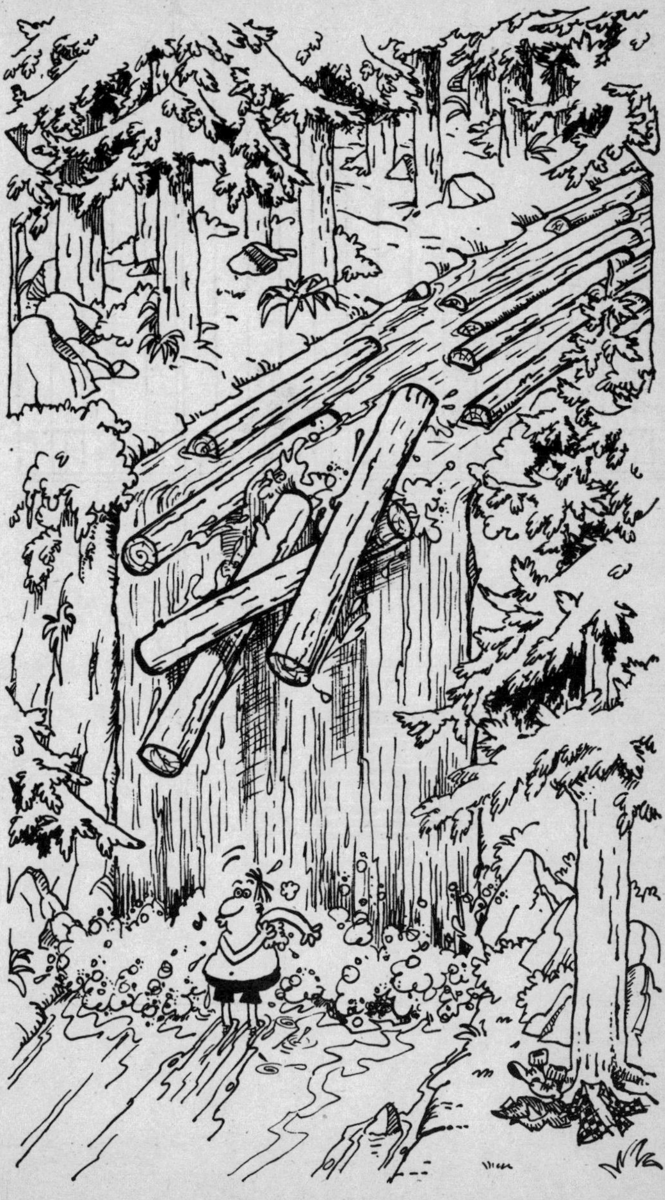

1

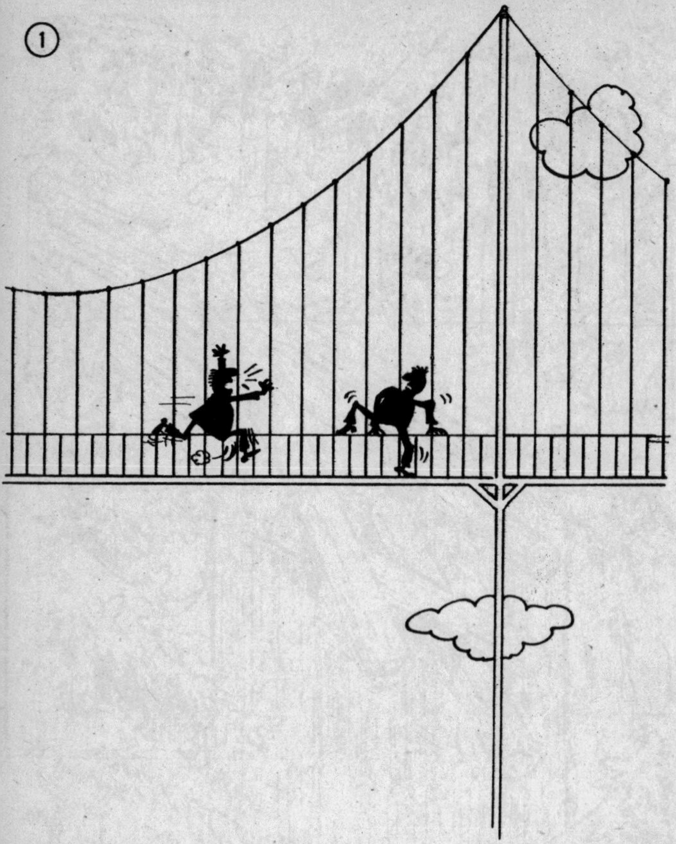

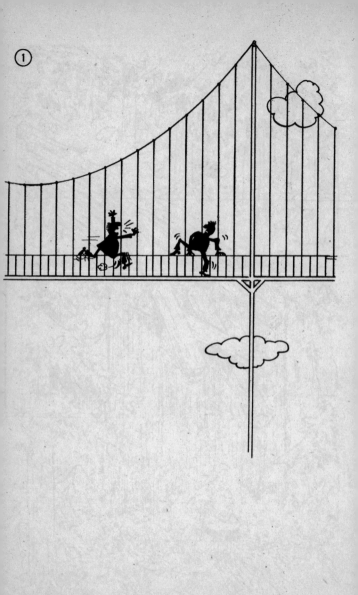

②

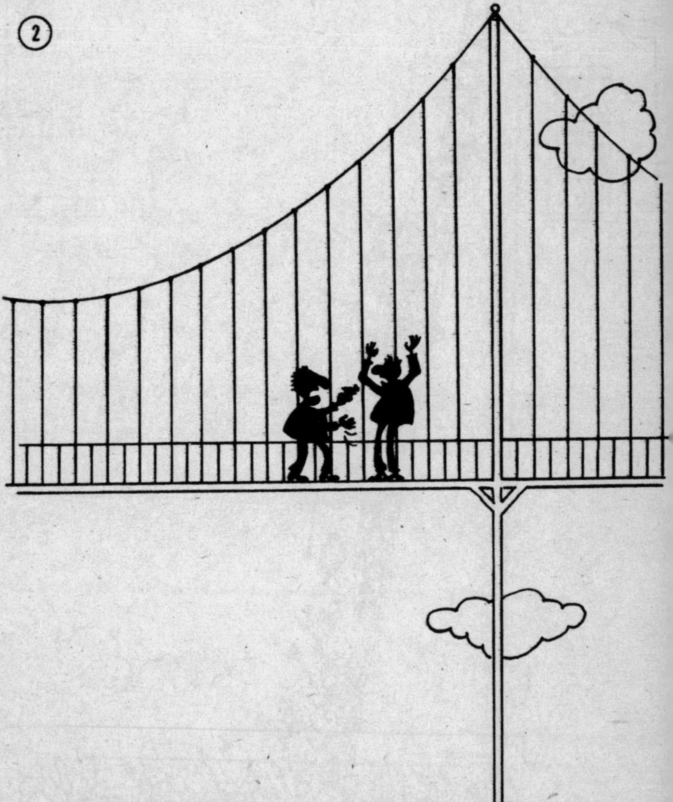

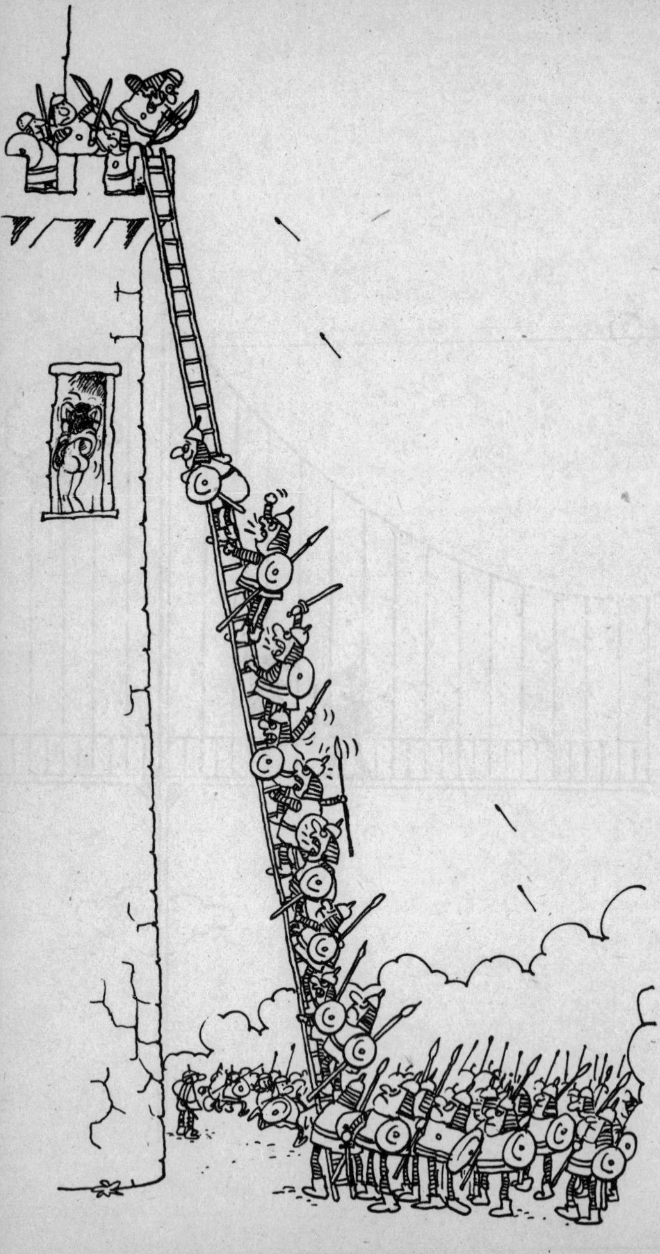

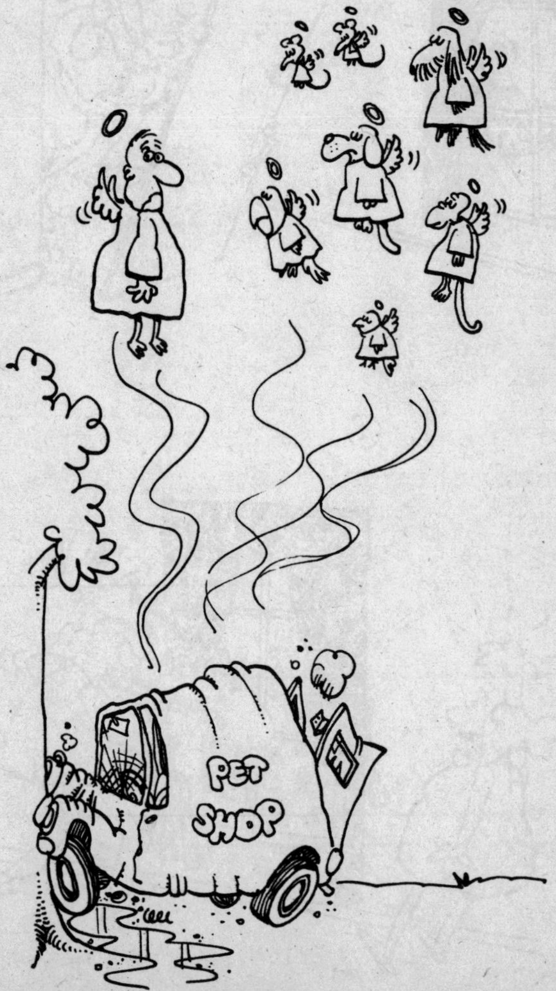
PET
SHOP

1

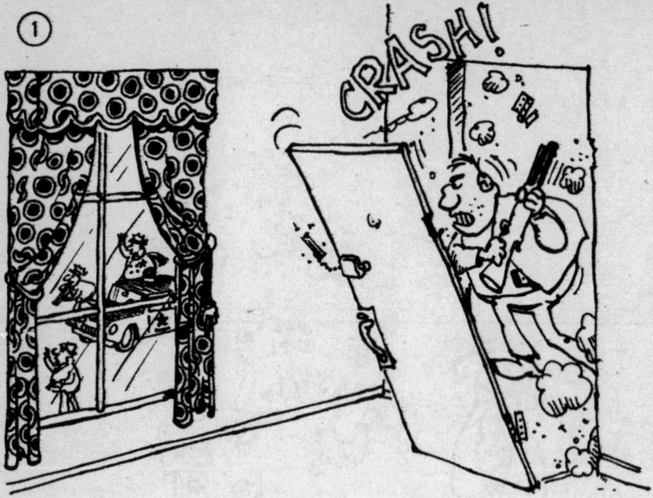
CRASH!

2

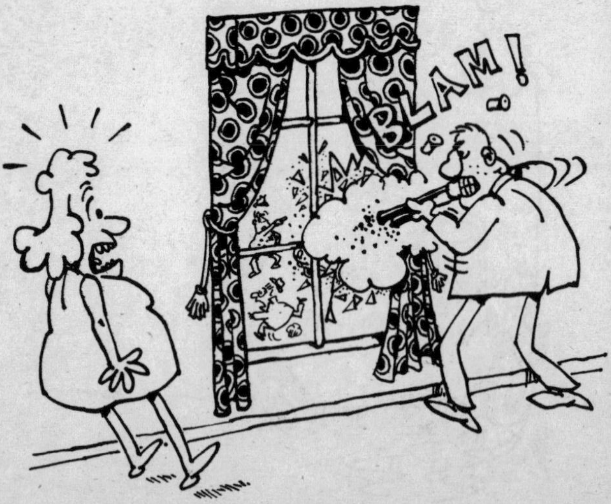
BLAM!

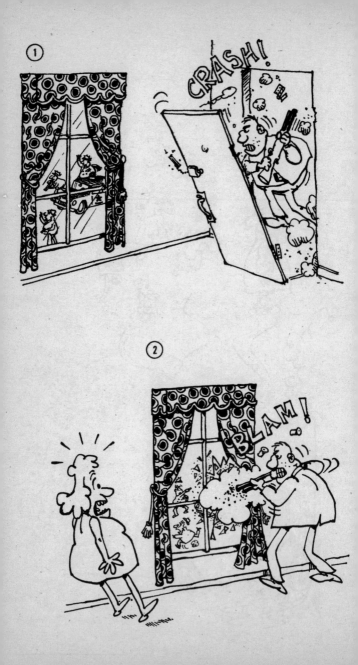

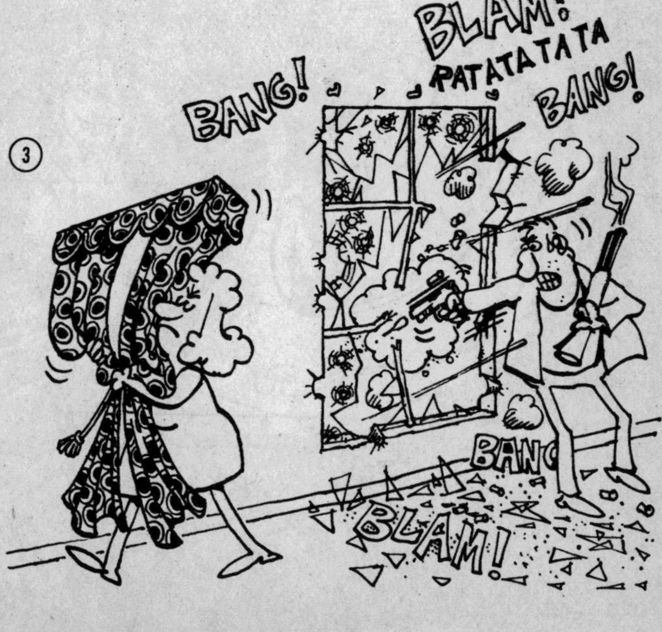
③
BANG!
BLAM!
RATATATATA
BANG!
BANG
BLAM!

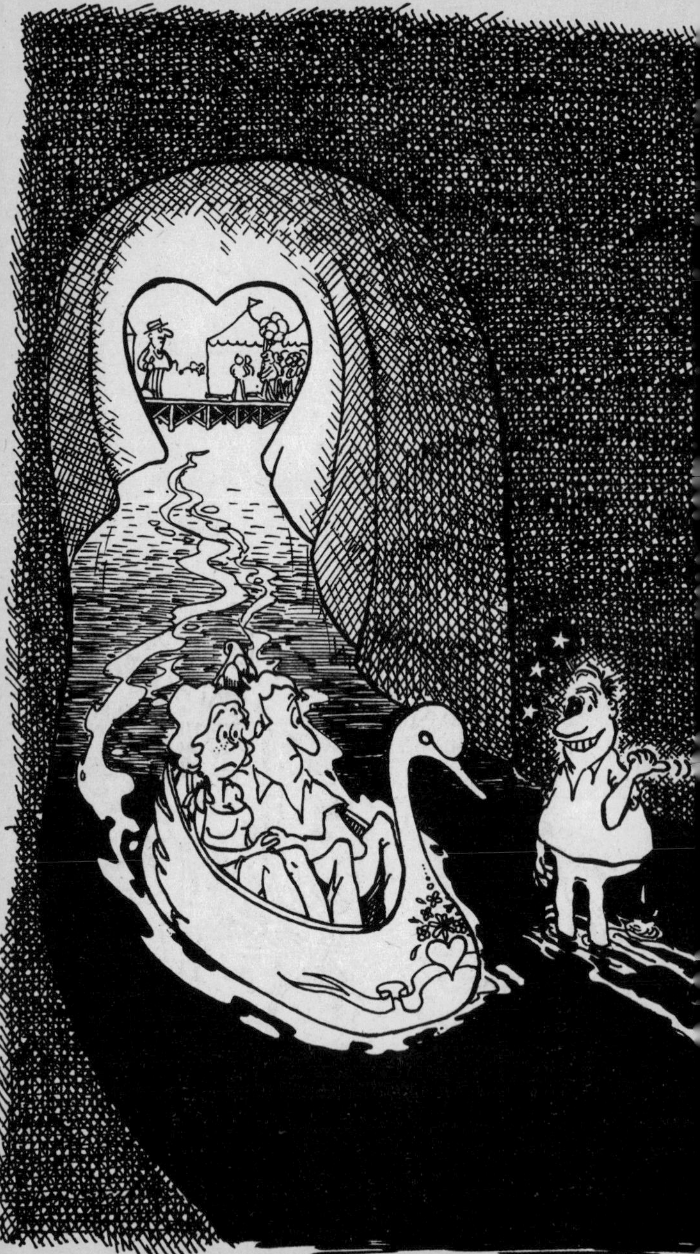

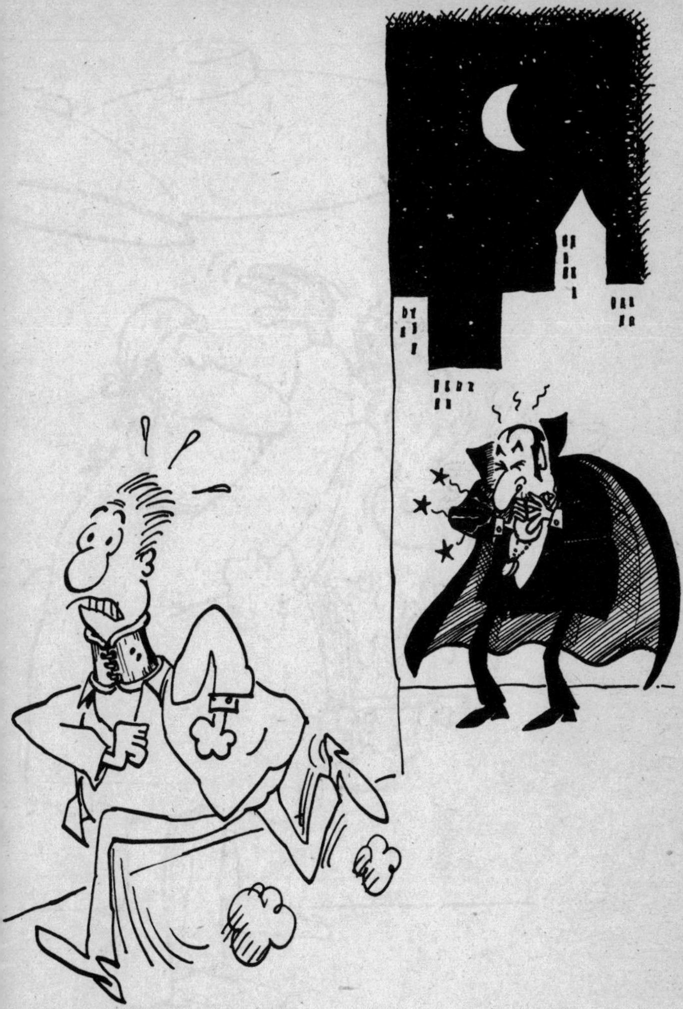

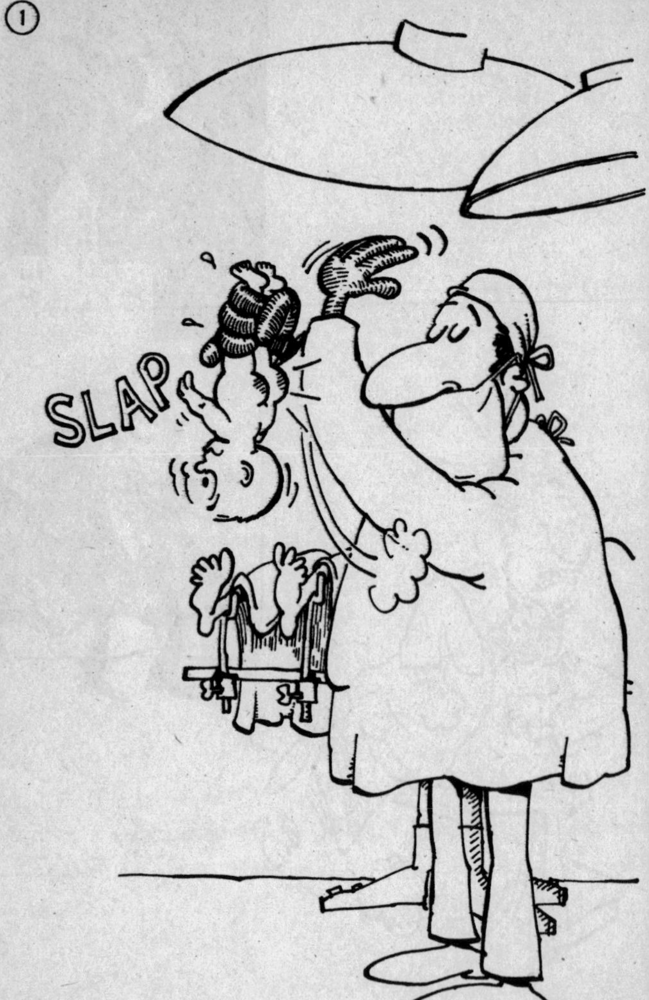
1
SLAP

②

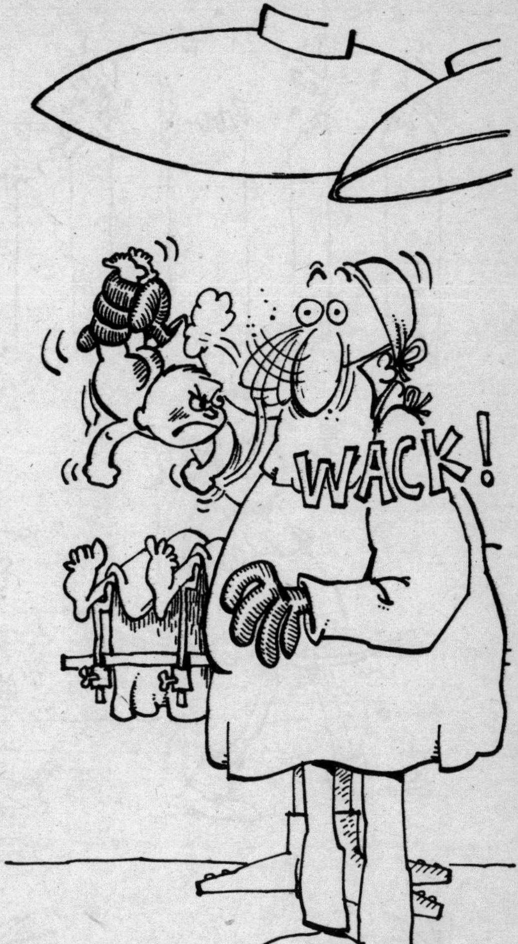
WACK!

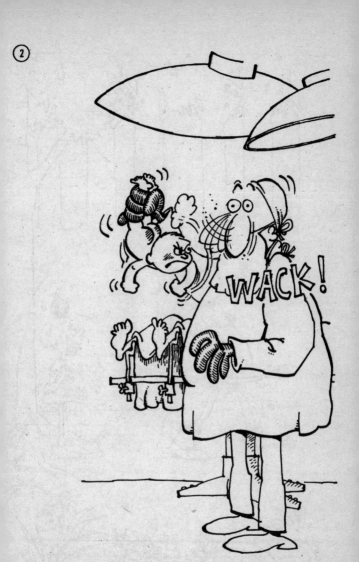

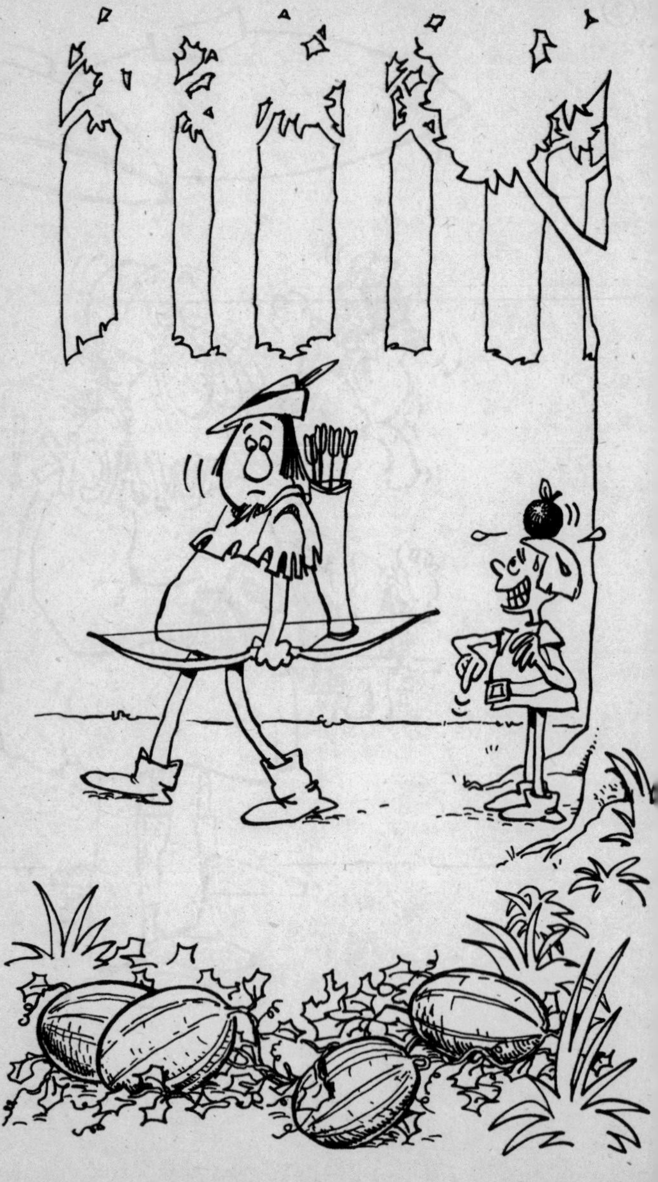

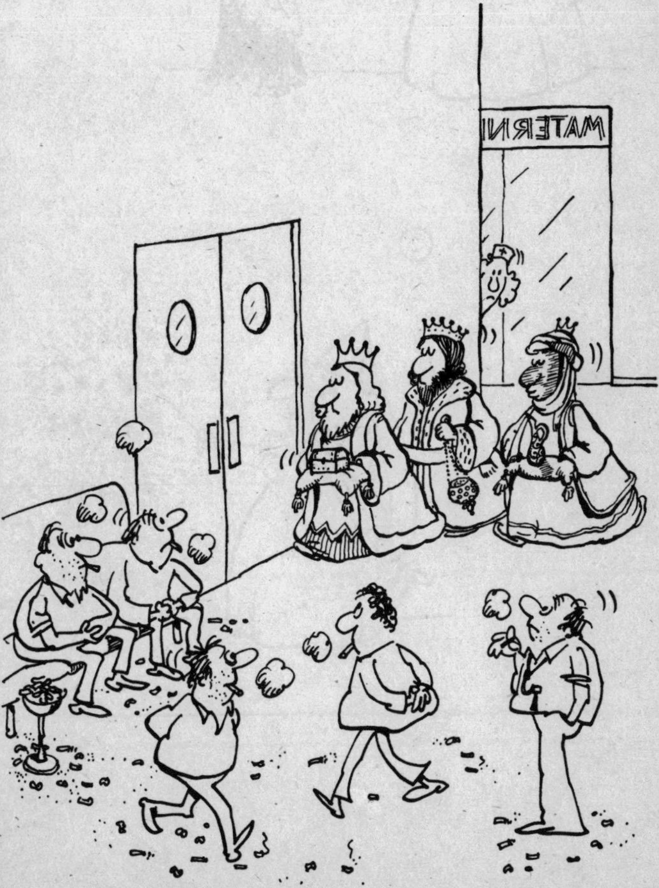
MATERNI

(1)

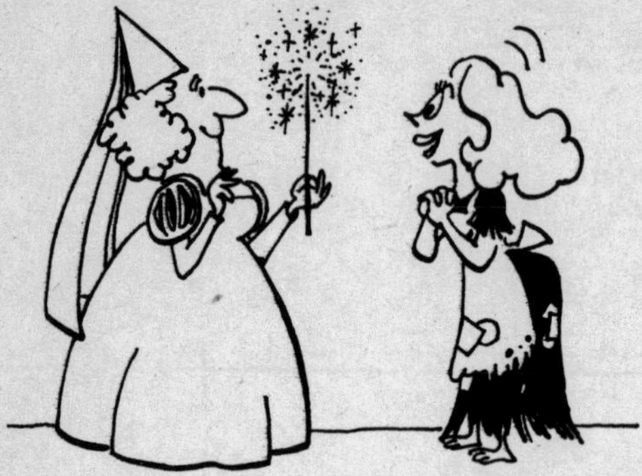

(2)

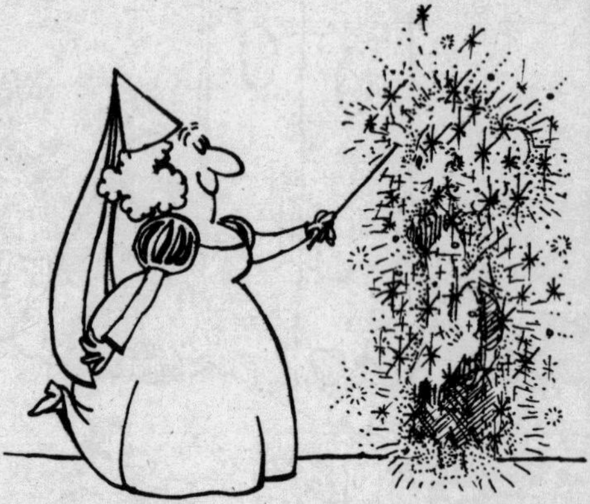

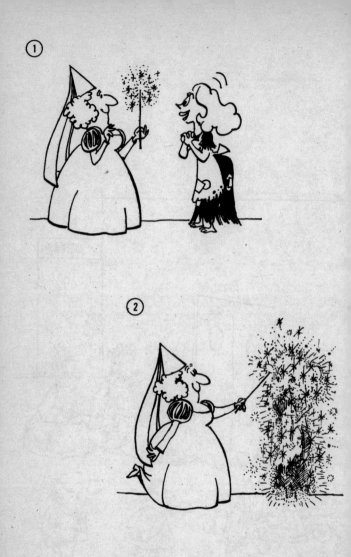

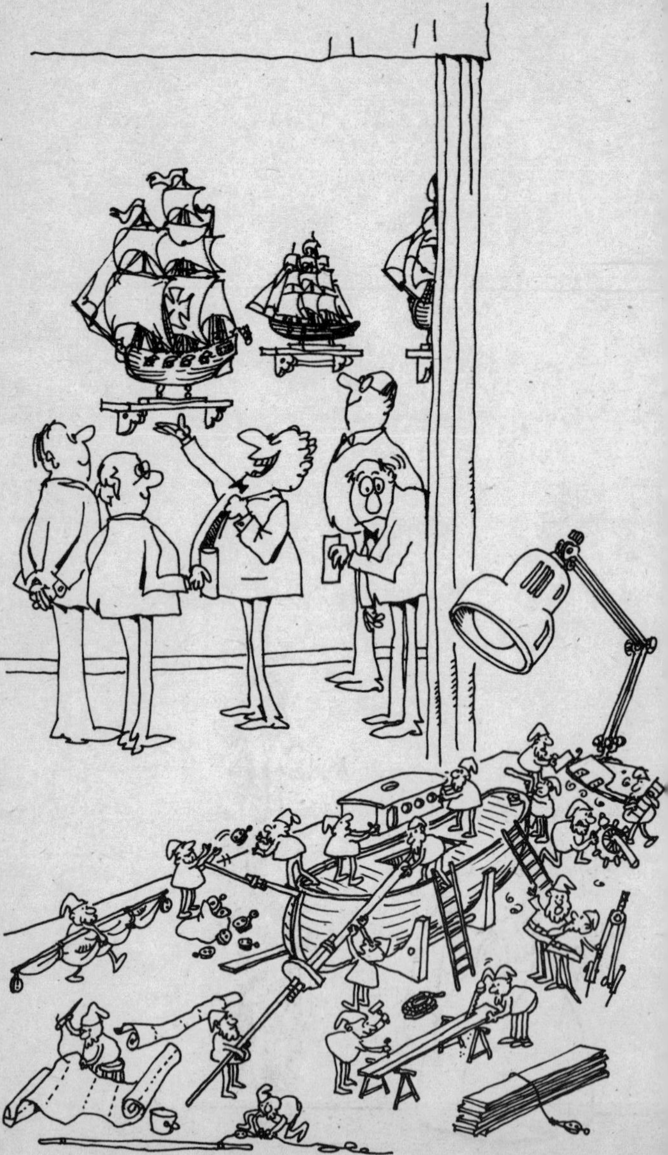

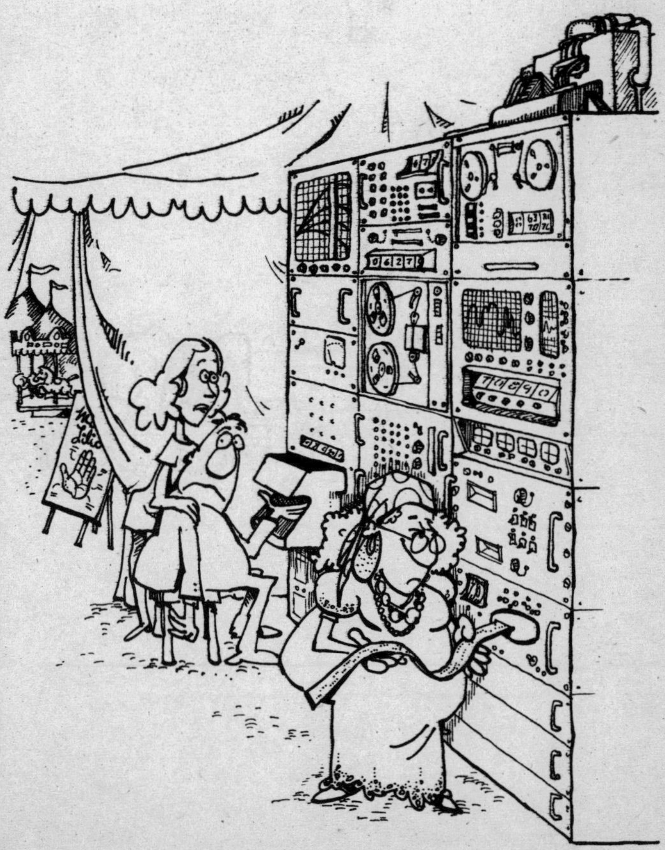

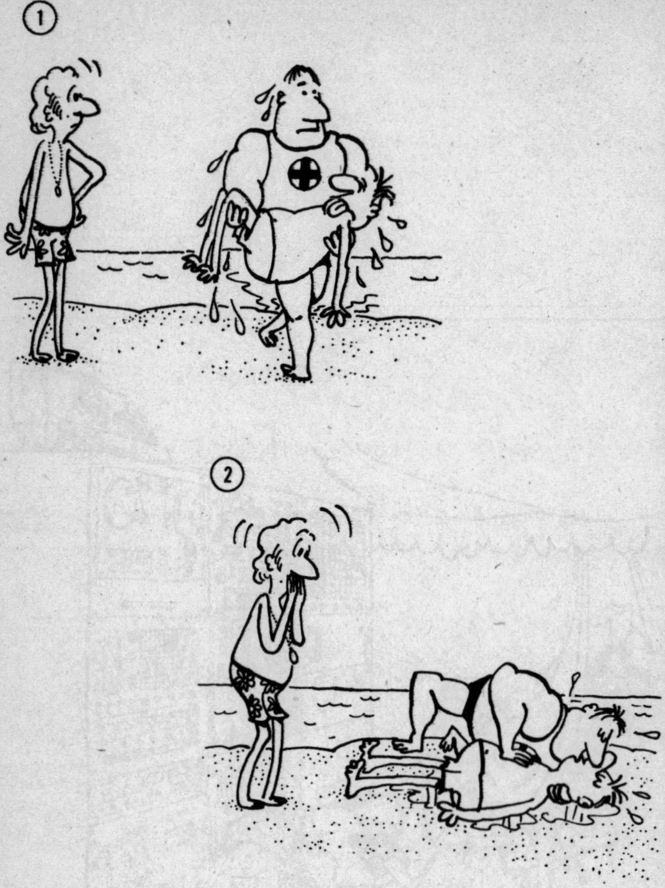
1
2

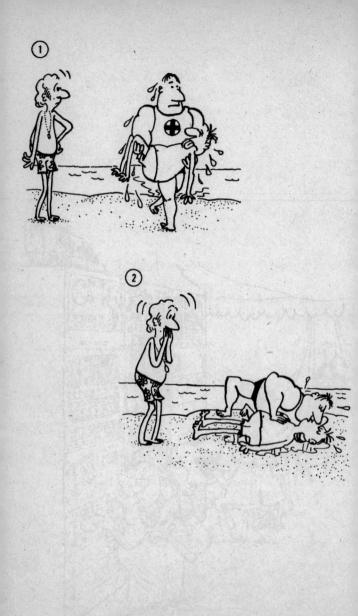

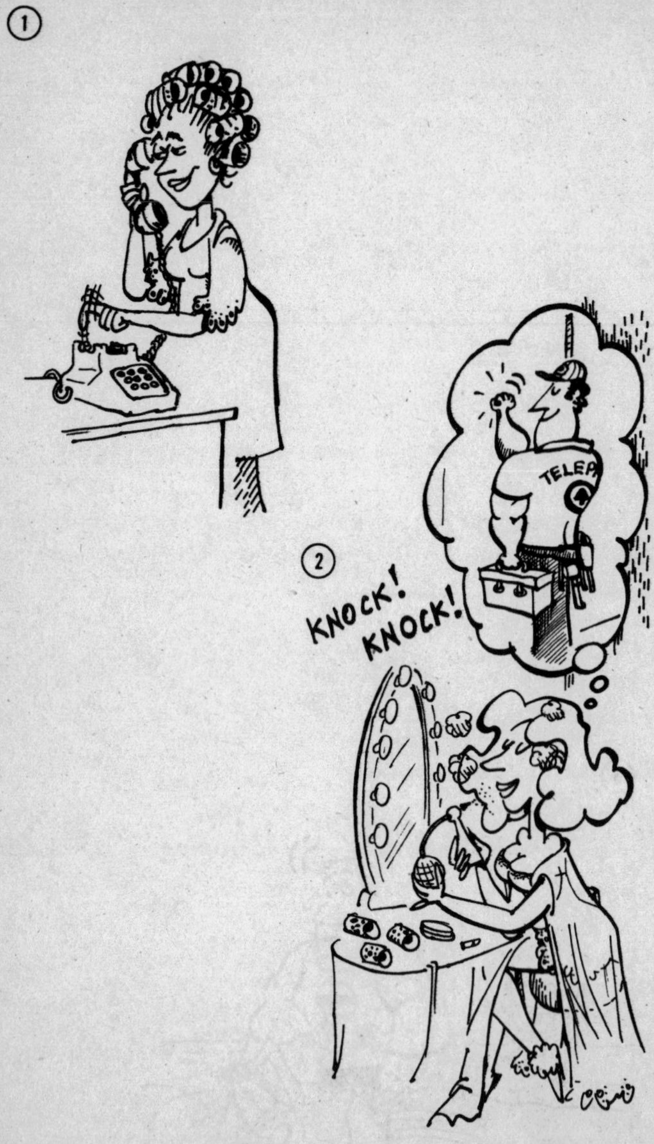
1
2
KNOCK! KNOCK!

3

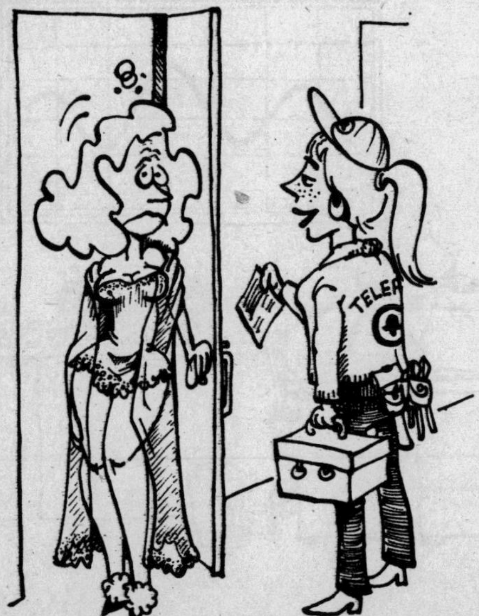
TELE

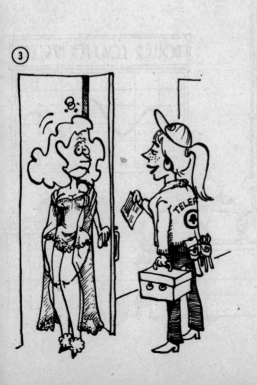

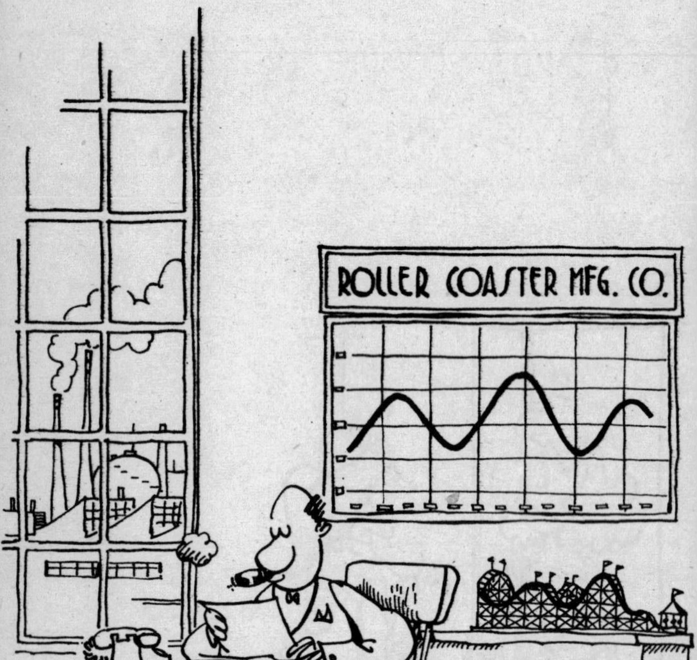
ROLLER COASTER MFG. CO.

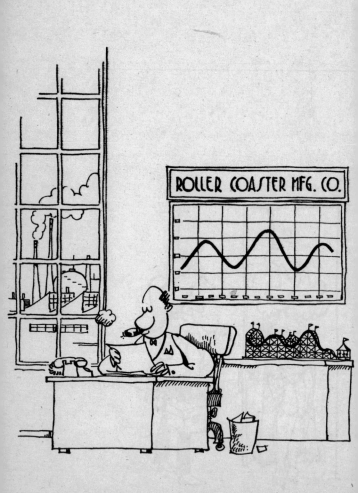

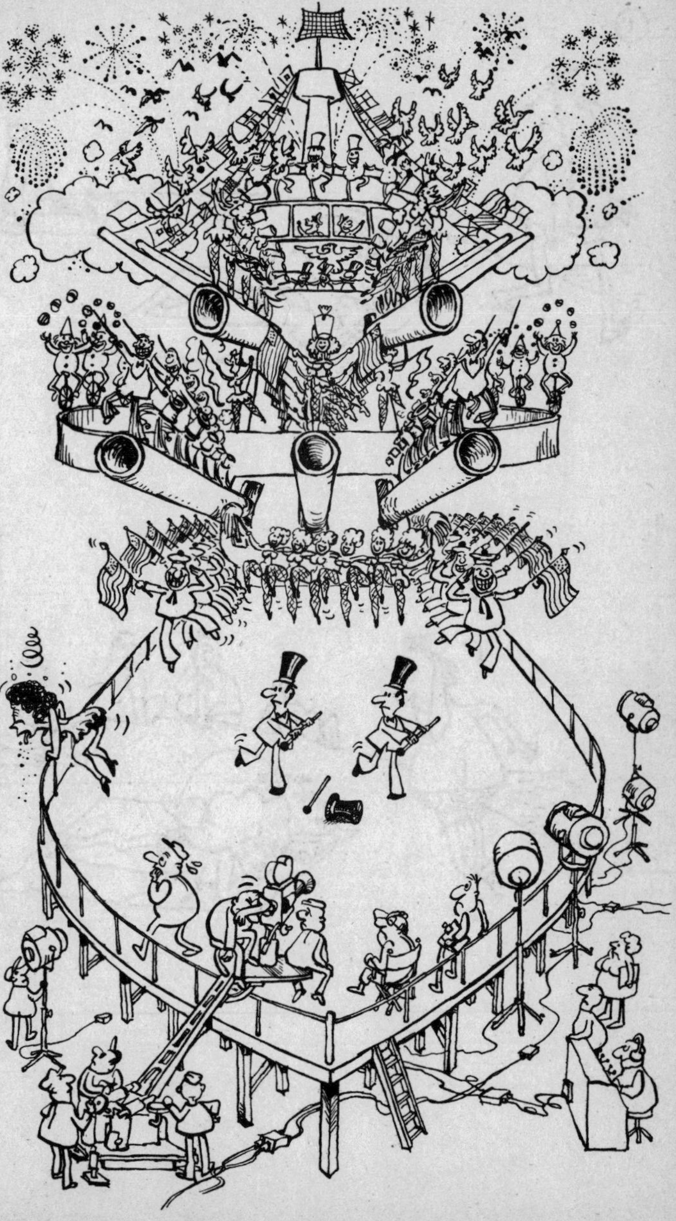

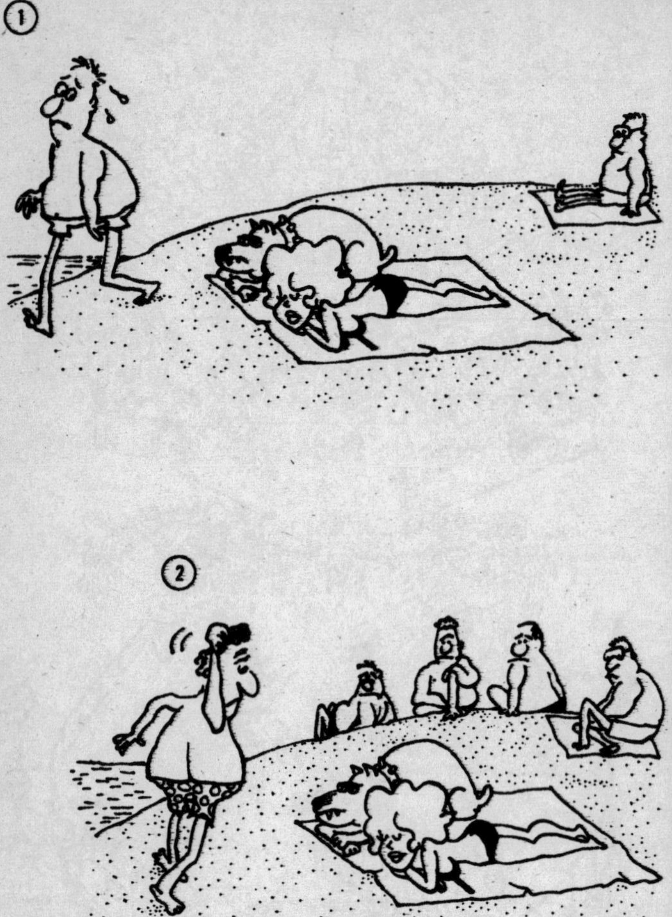
1
2

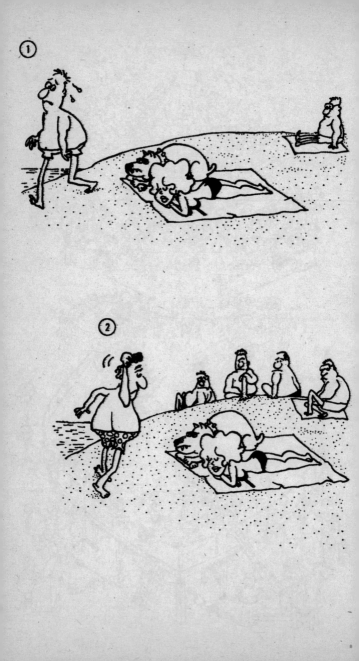

1

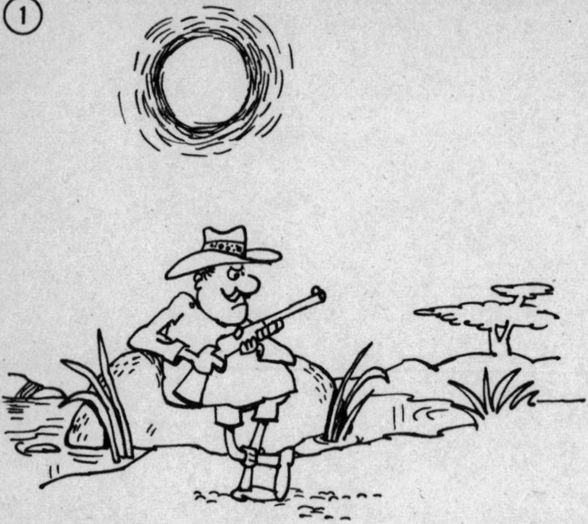

2

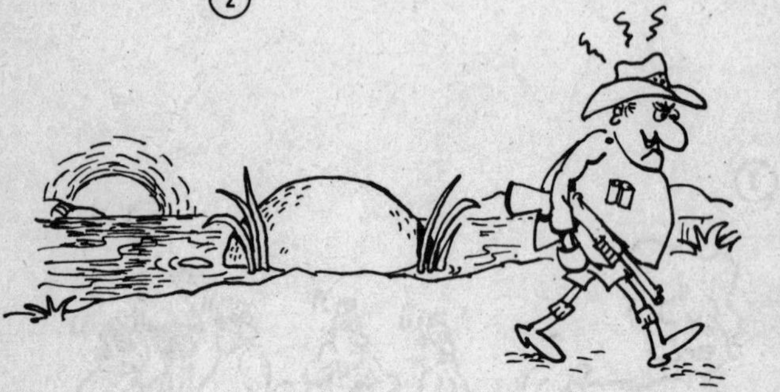

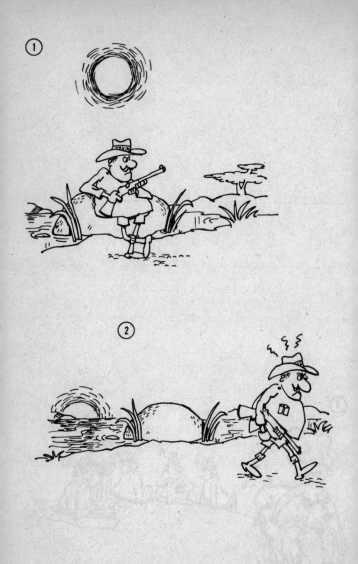

③

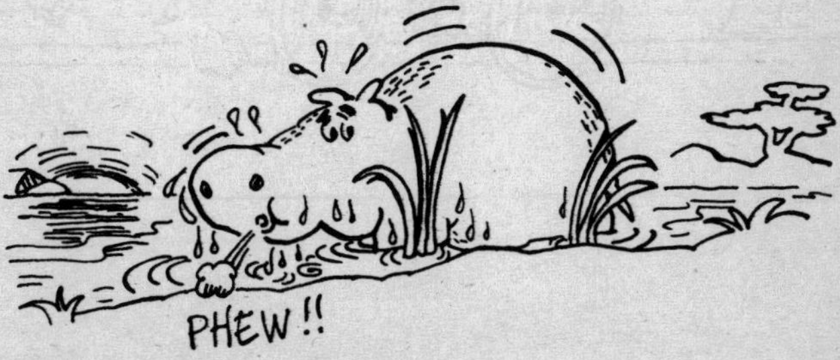
PHEW!!

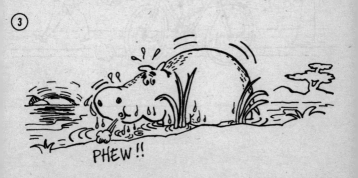

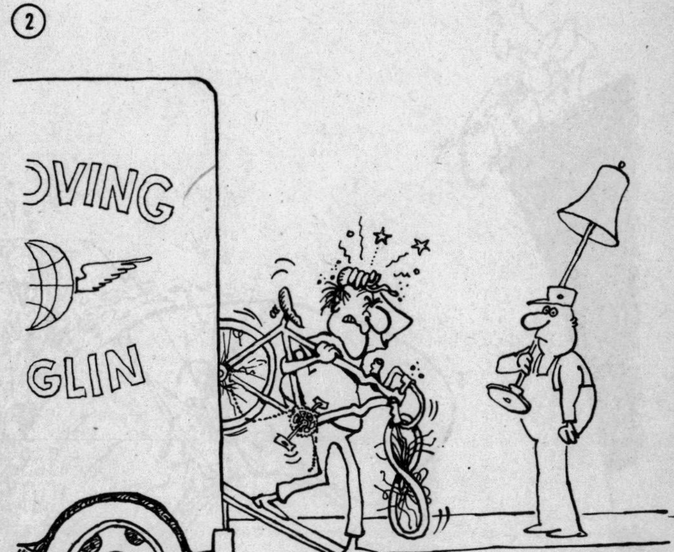

2
OVING
GLIN

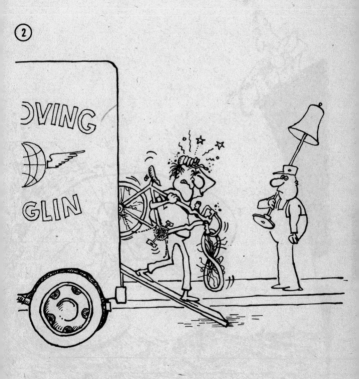

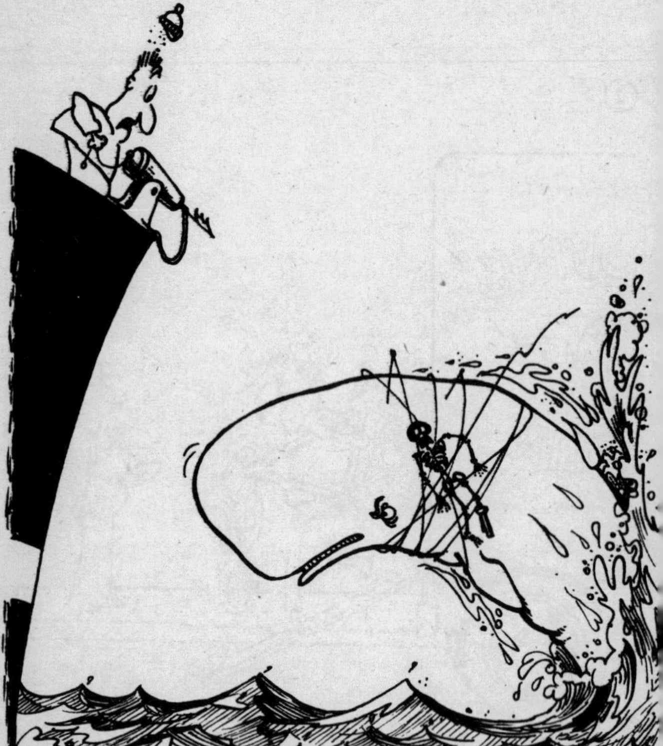

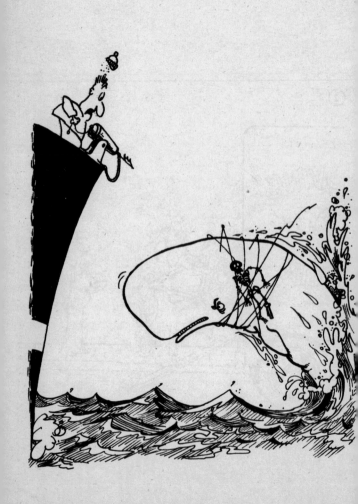

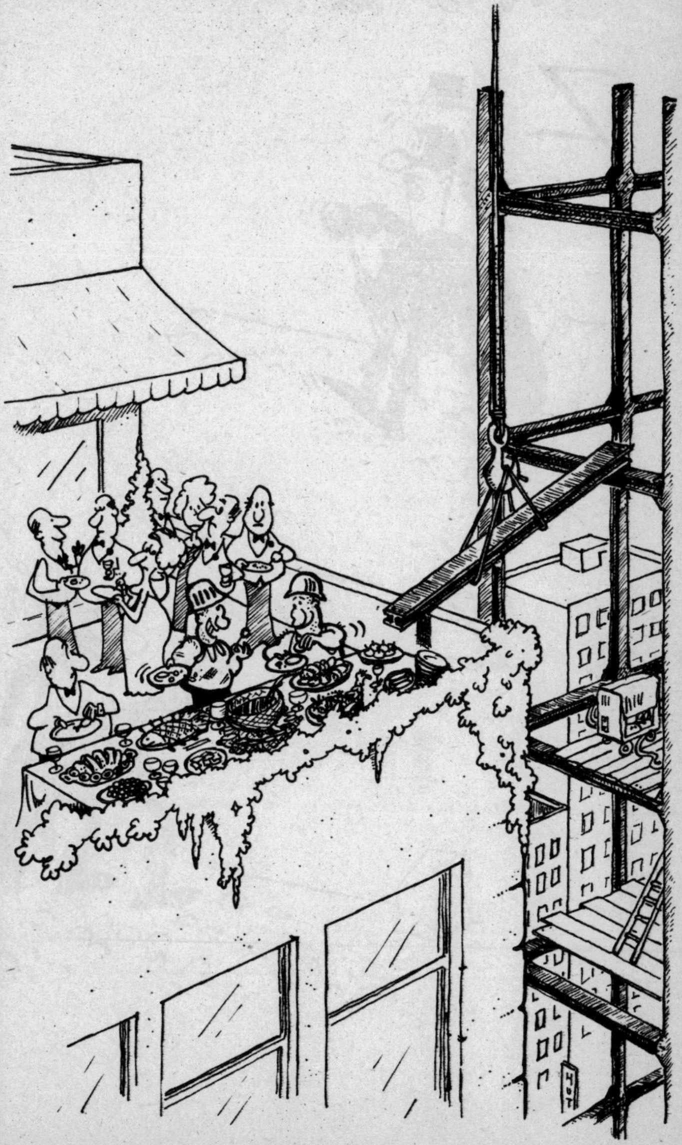

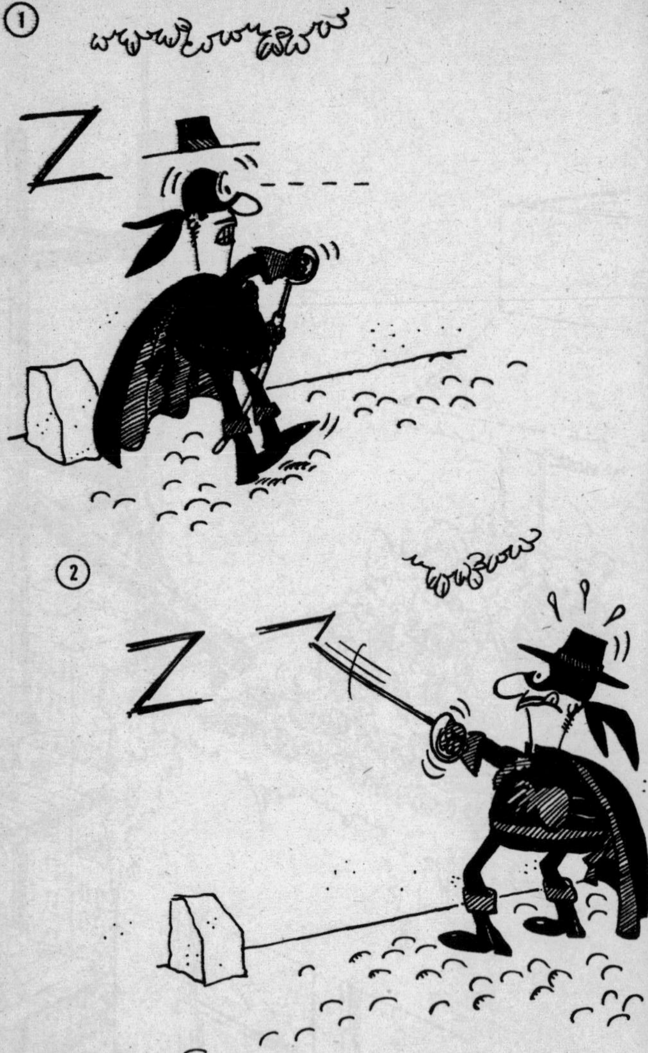
1
Z
2
Z

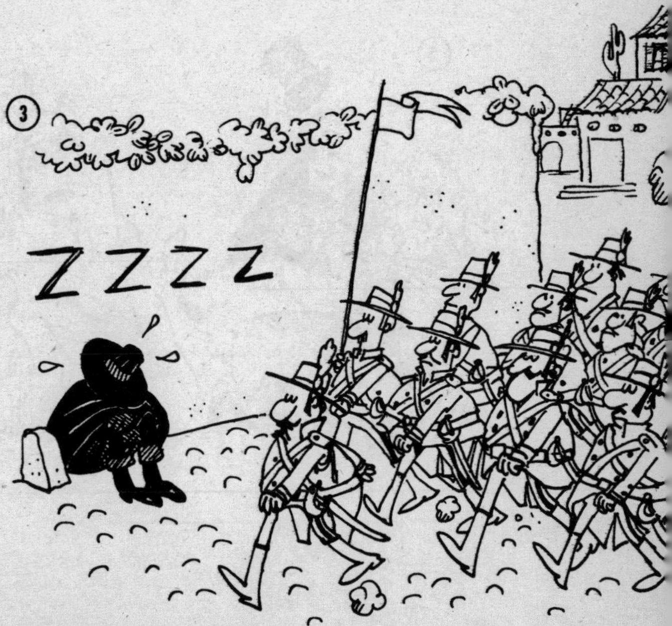
ZZZZ

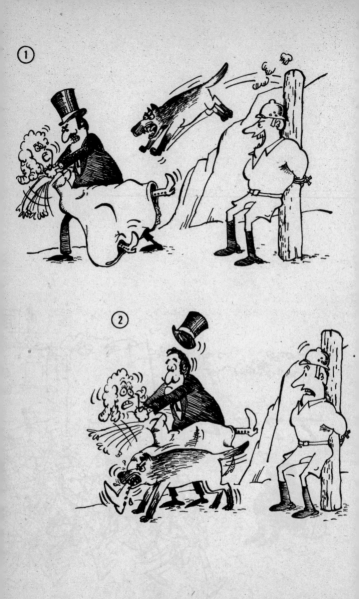

1

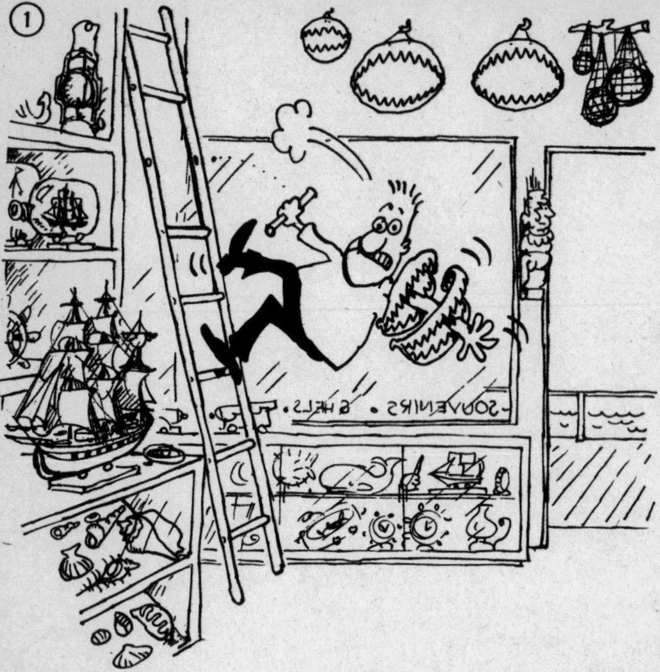
SOUVENIRS • SHELLS •

2

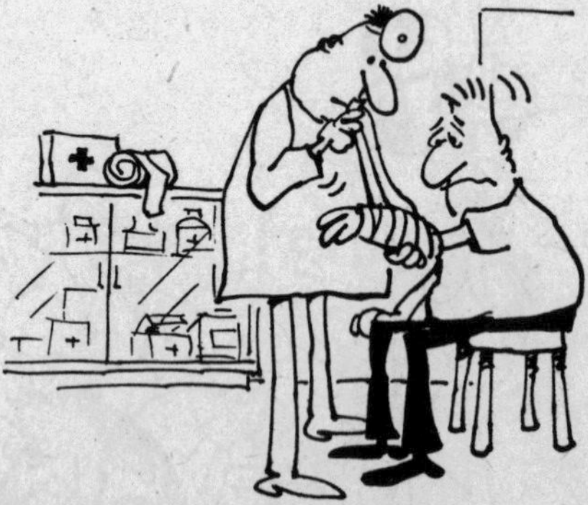

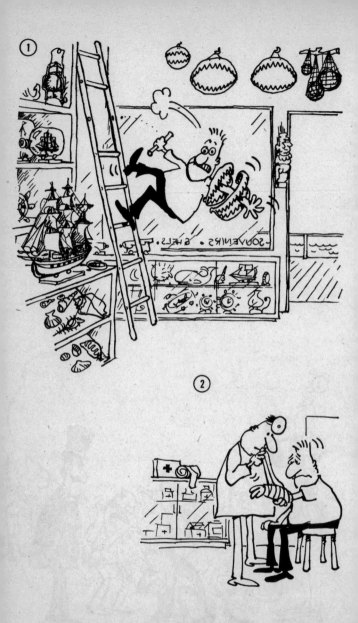

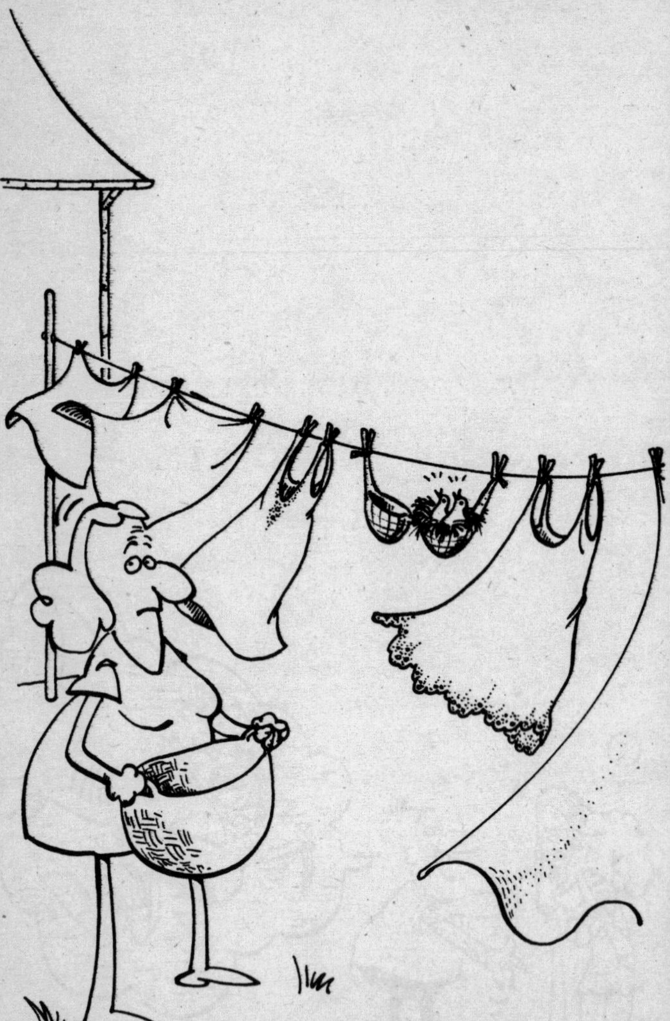

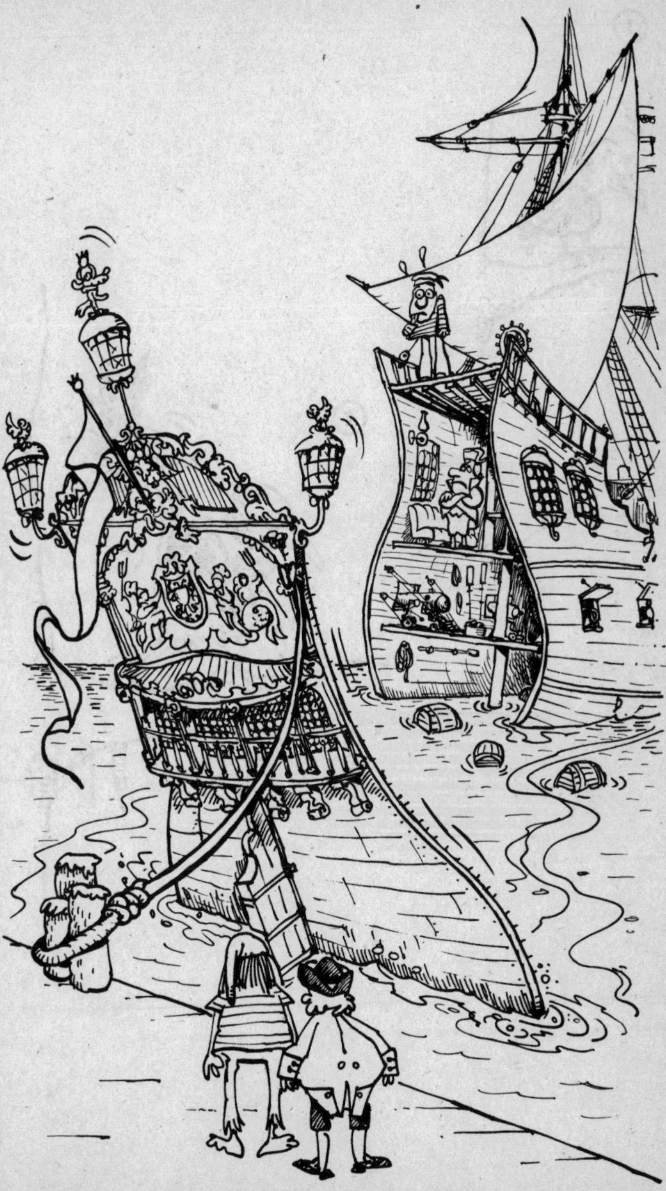

1

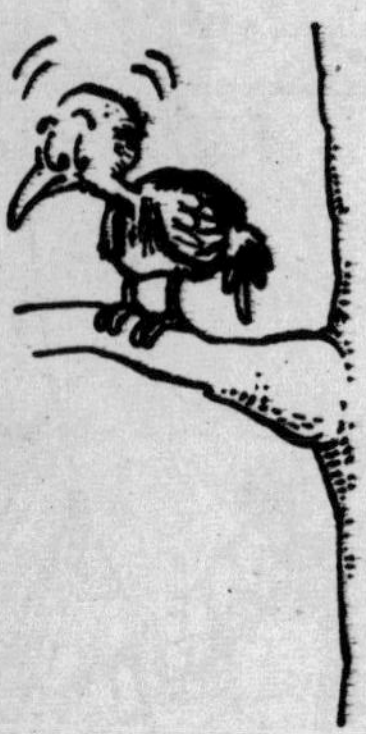

2

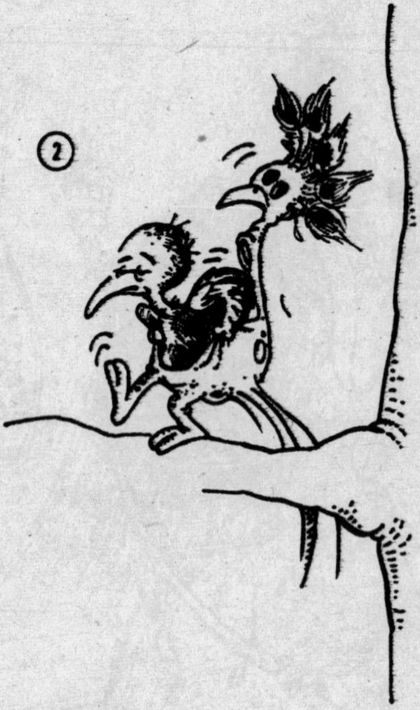

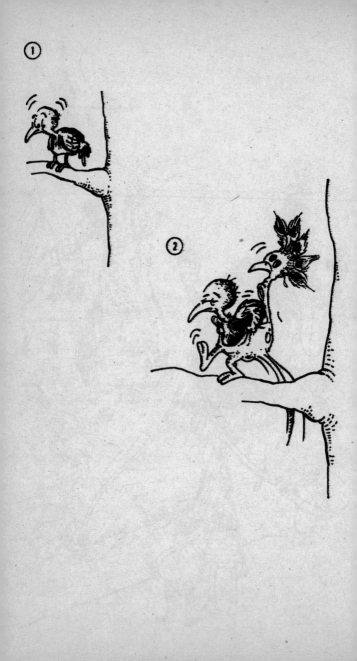

③

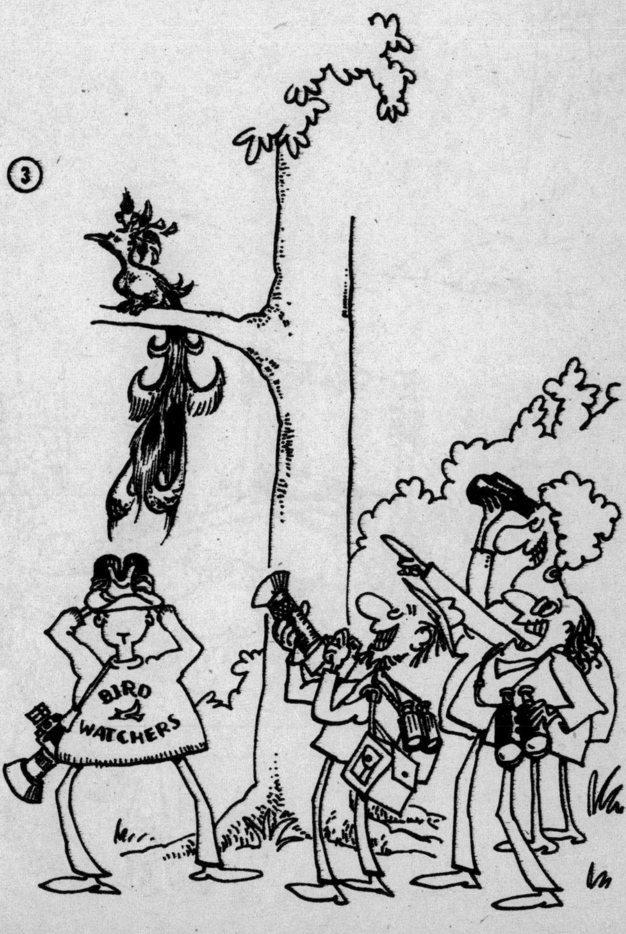
BIRD
WATCHERS

1

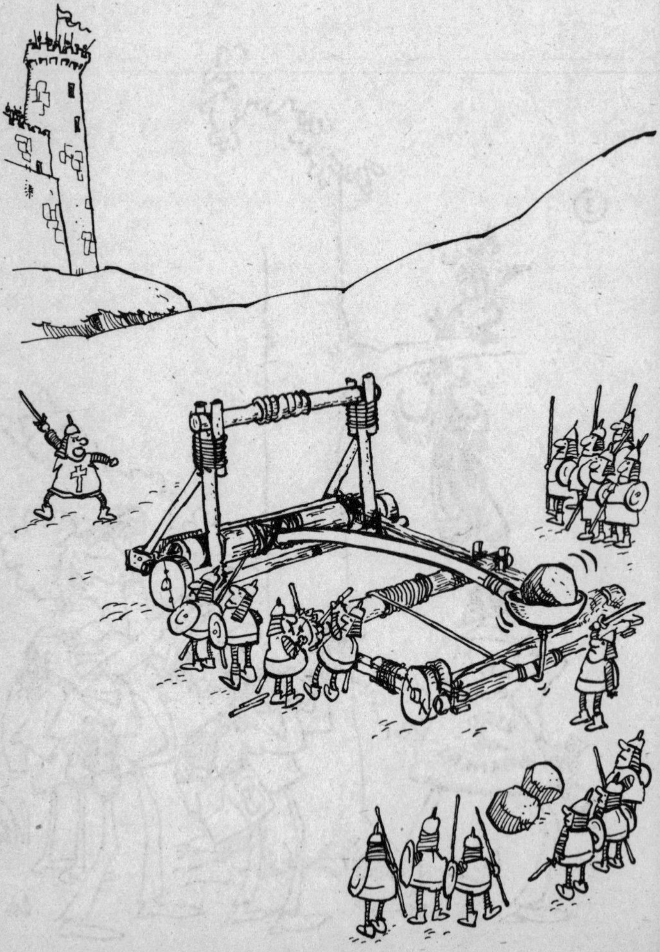

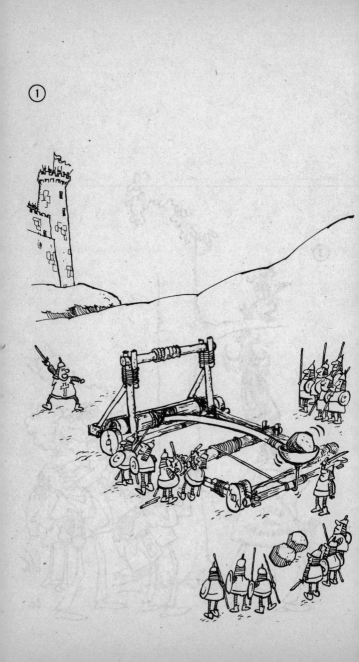

2

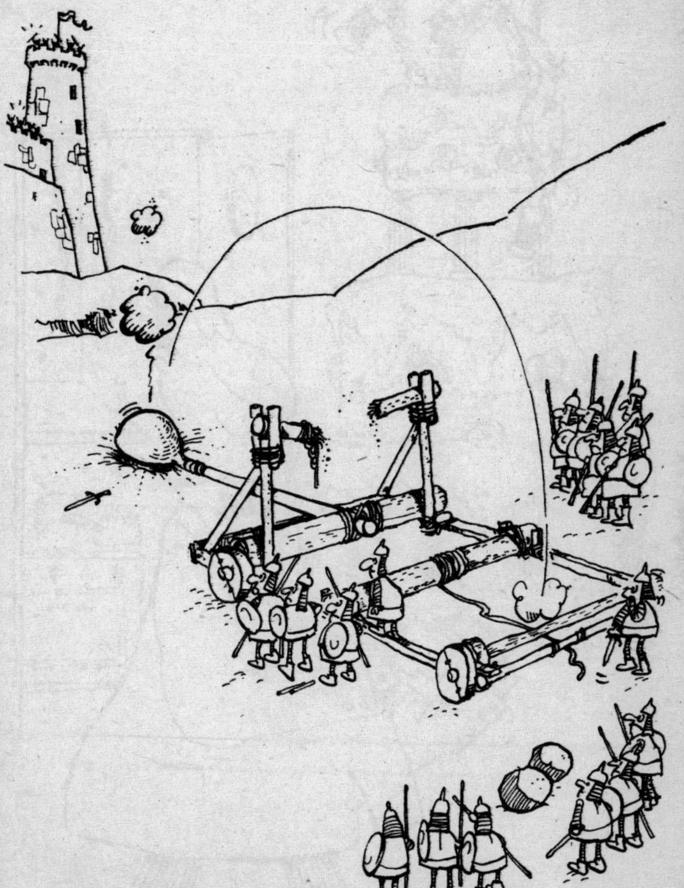

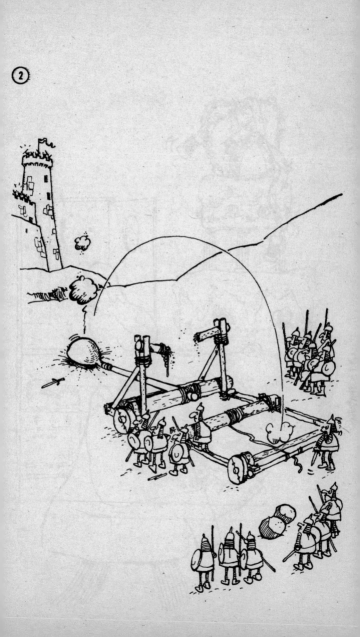

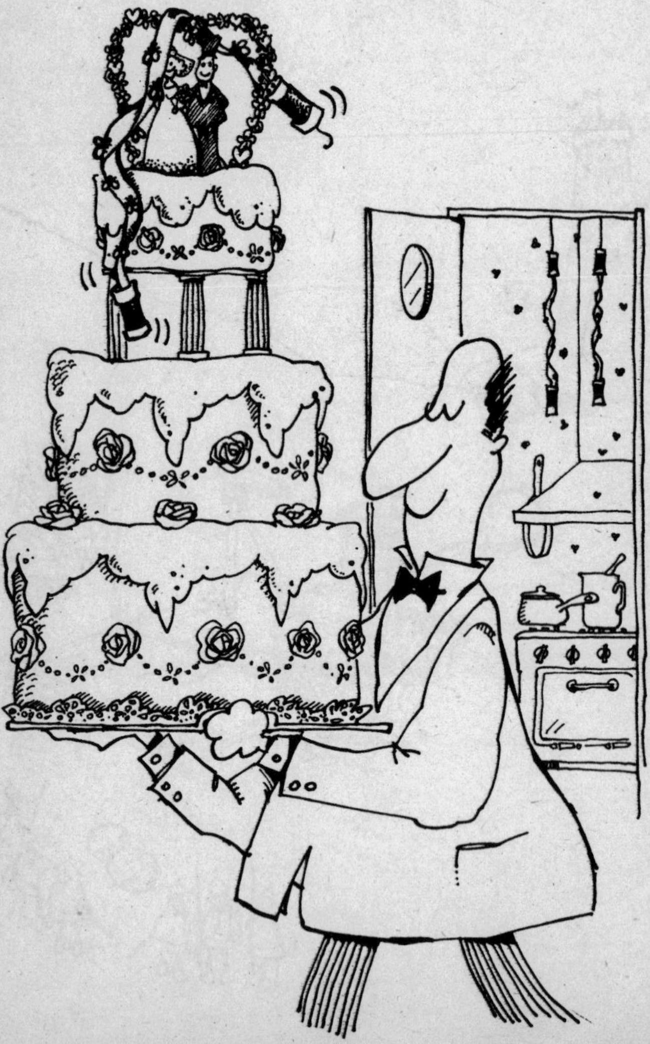

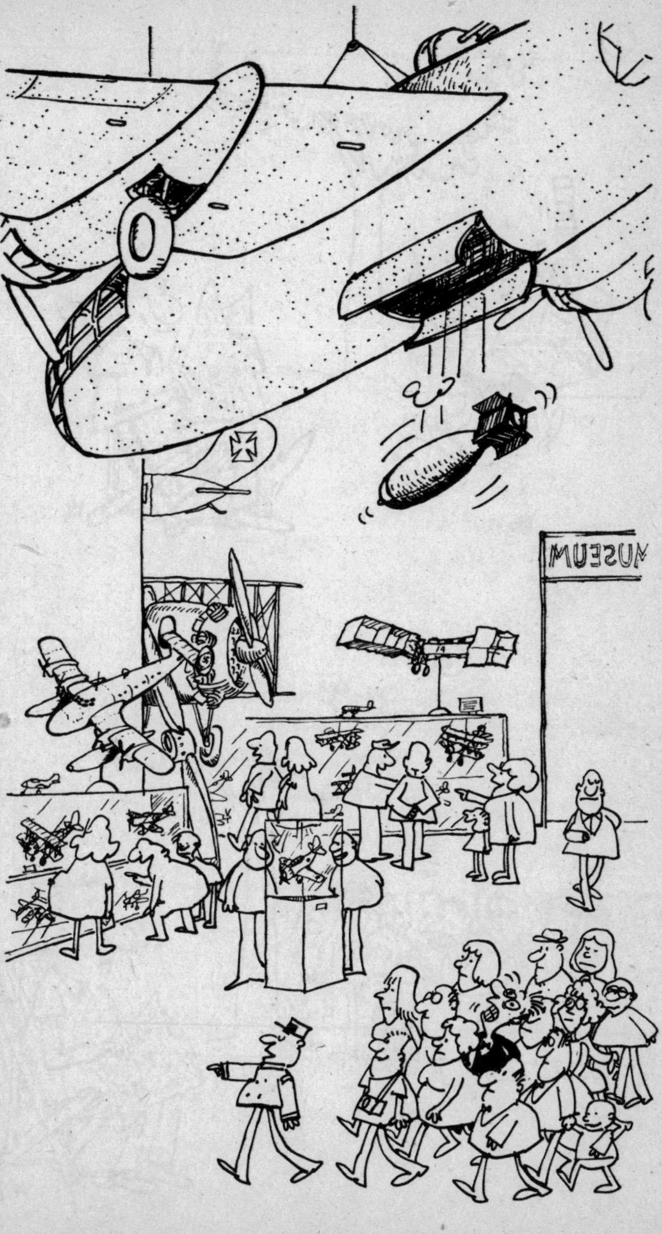
MUSEUM

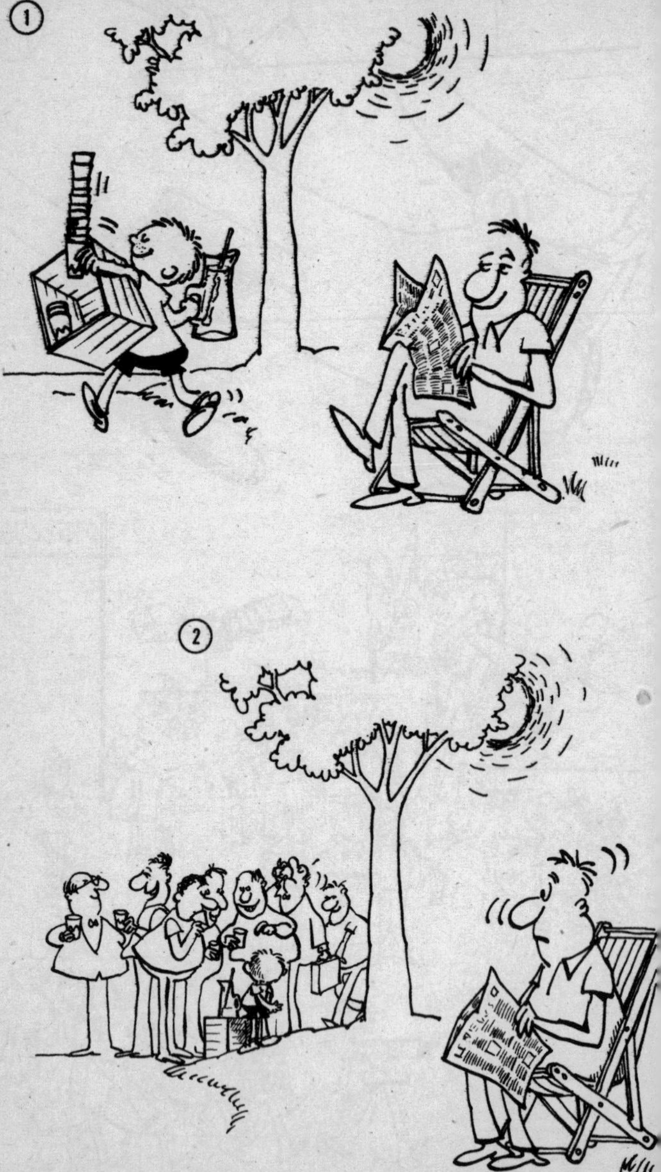

3

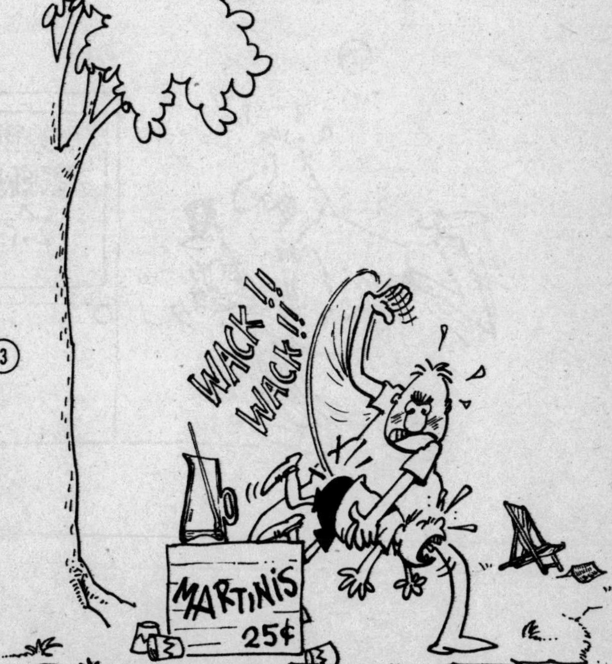
WACK!!
WACK!!
MARTINIS
25¢

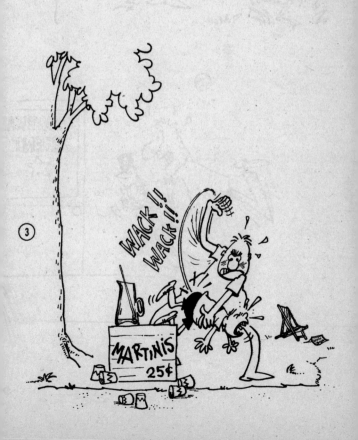

1

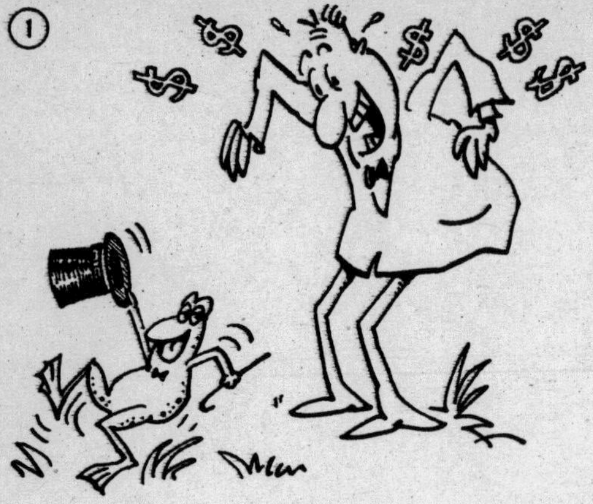

2

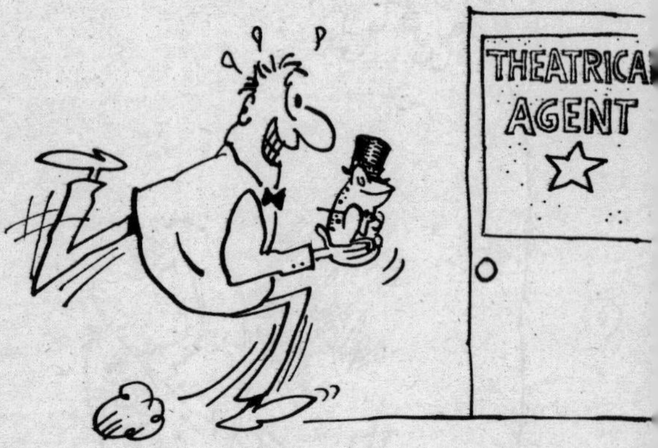
THEATRICAL
AGENT

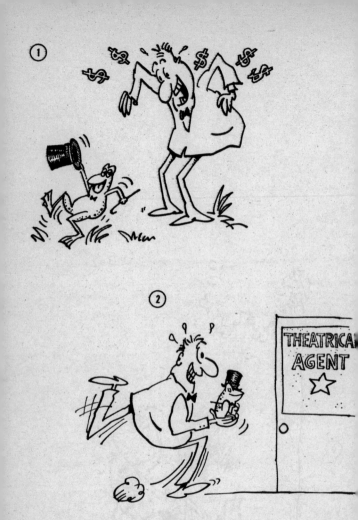

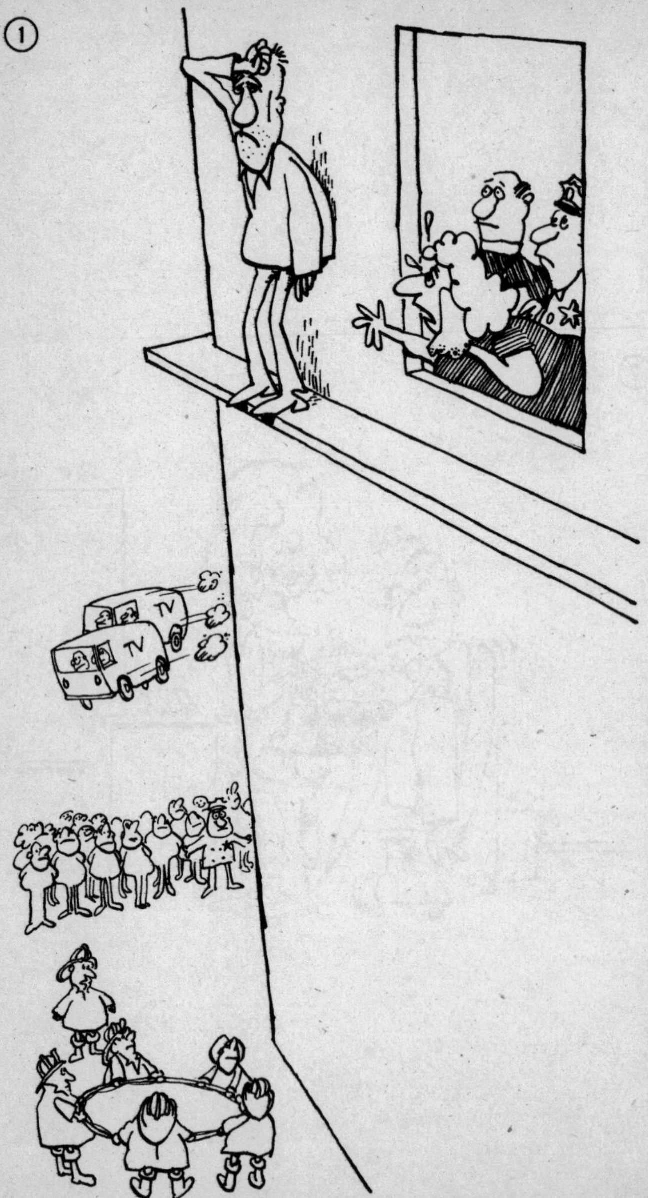

1
TV
TV

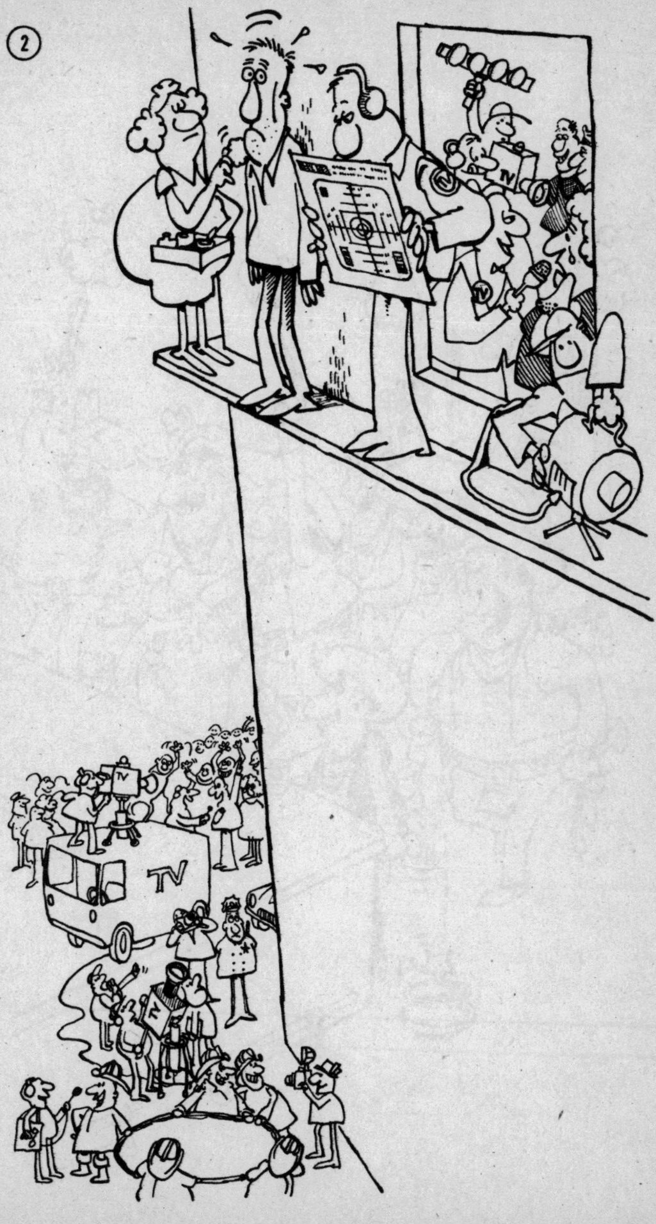
TV

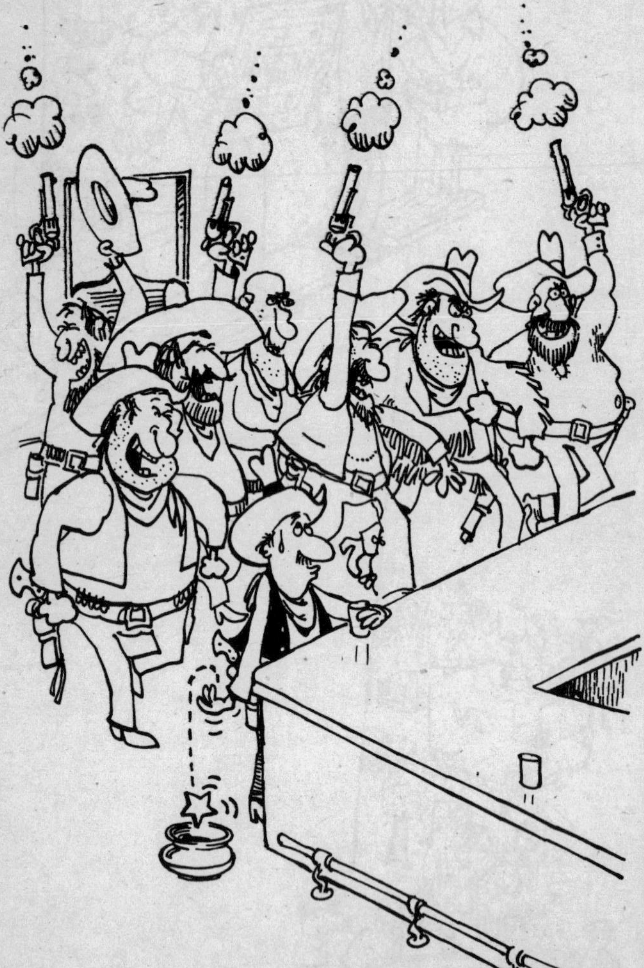

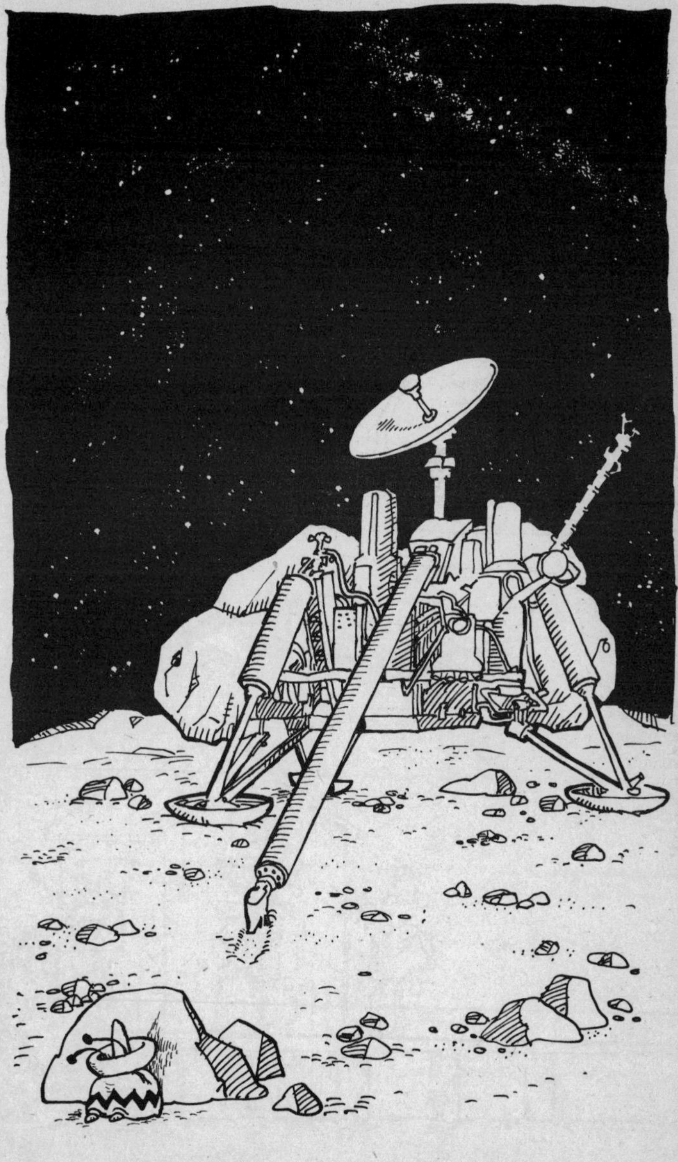

1

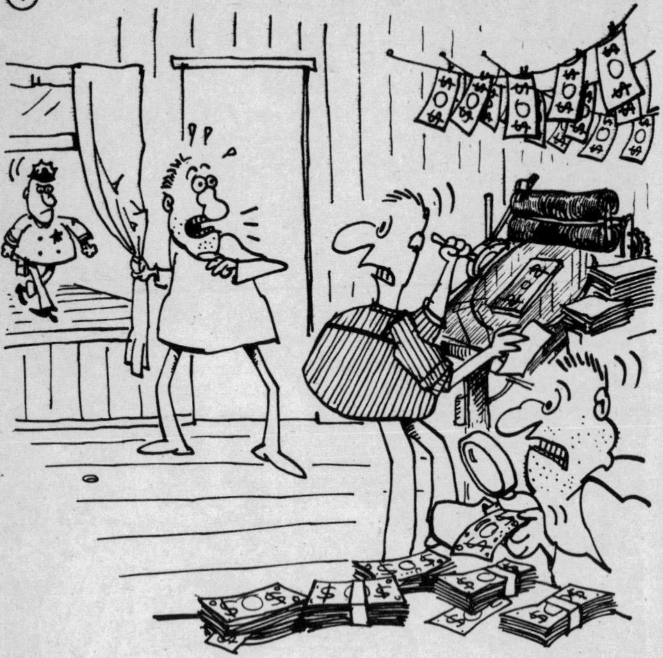

2

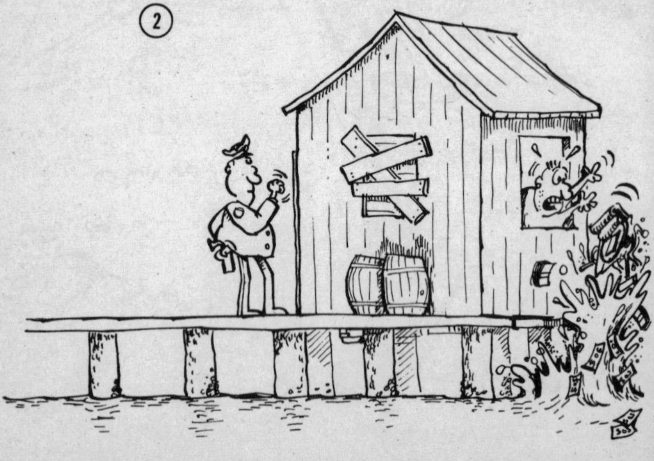

3

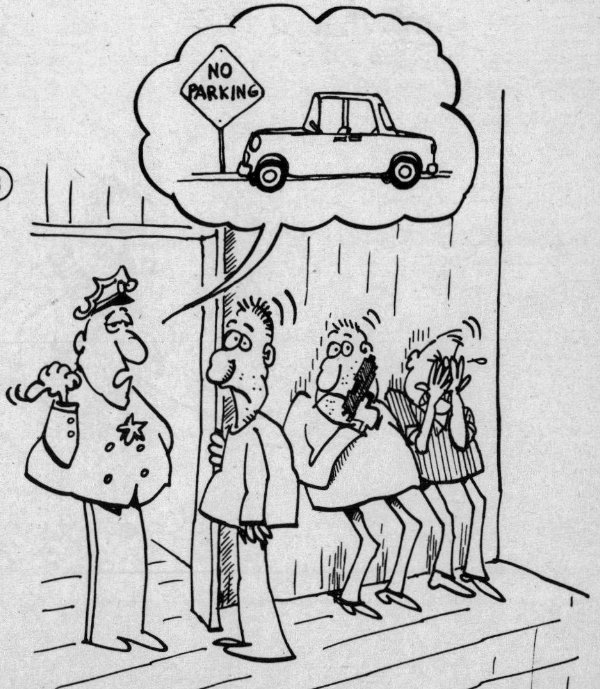
NO PARKING

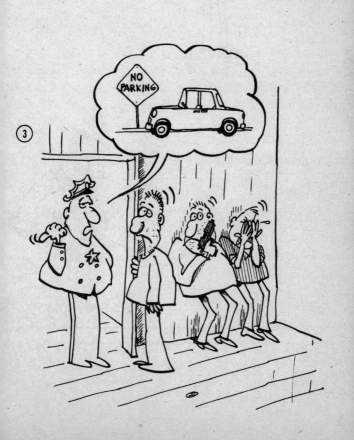

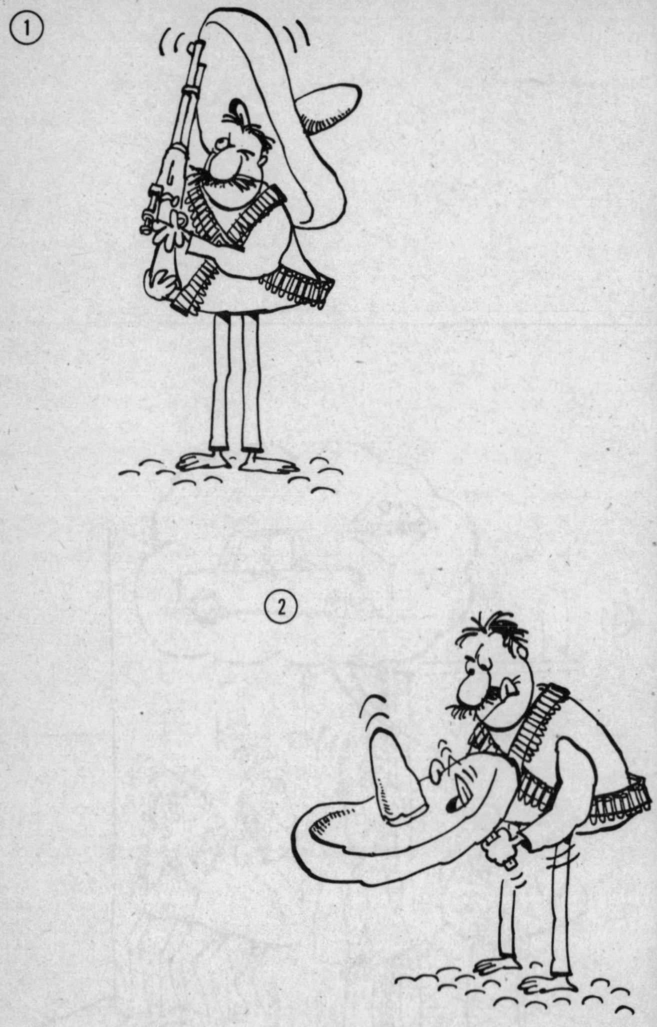
1
2

③

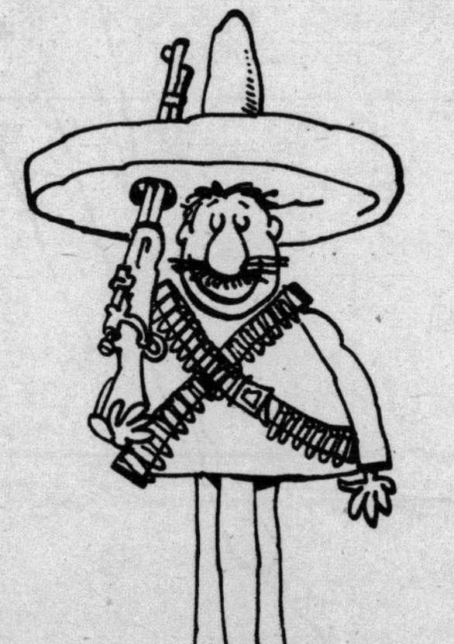

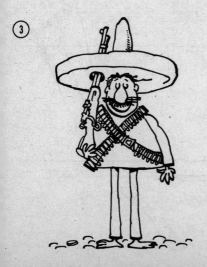

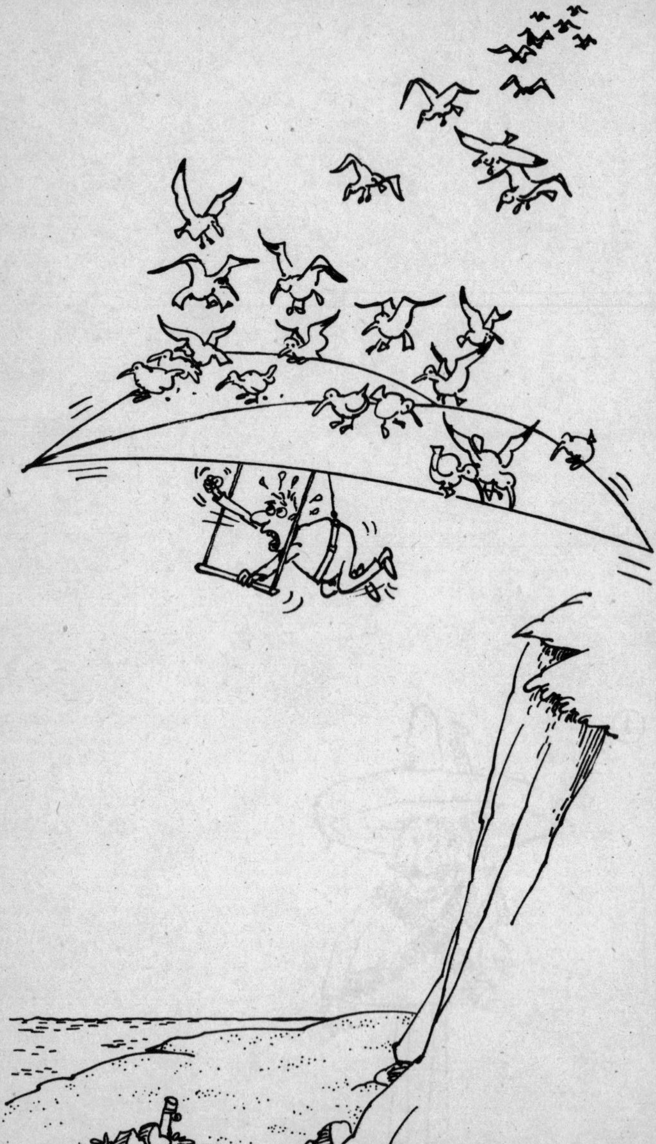

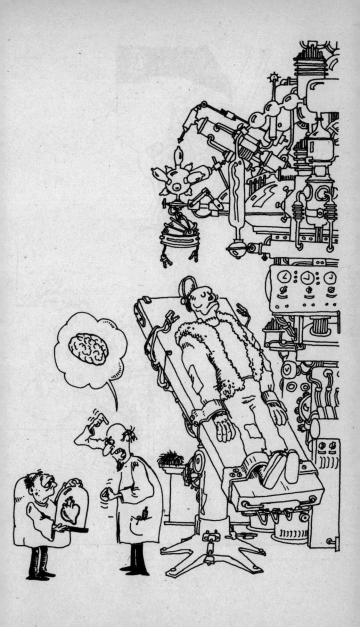

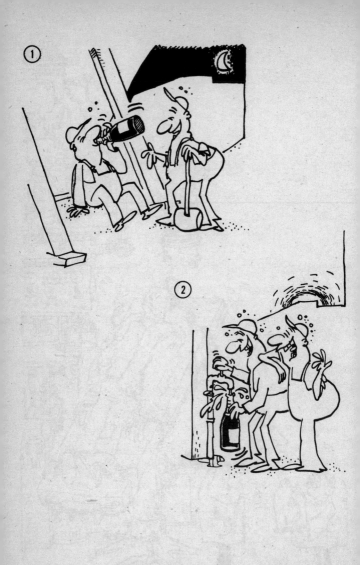

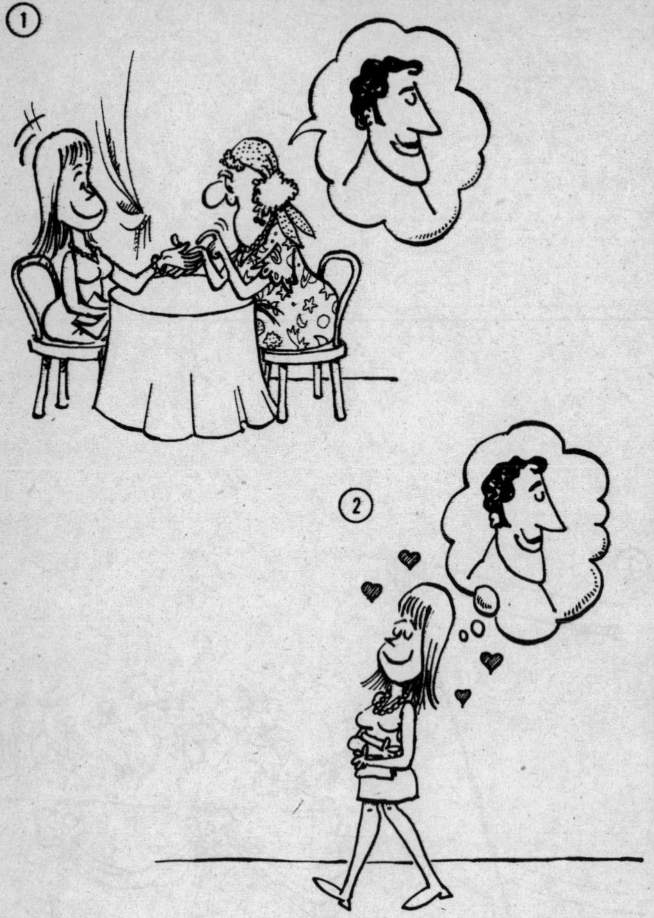
1
2

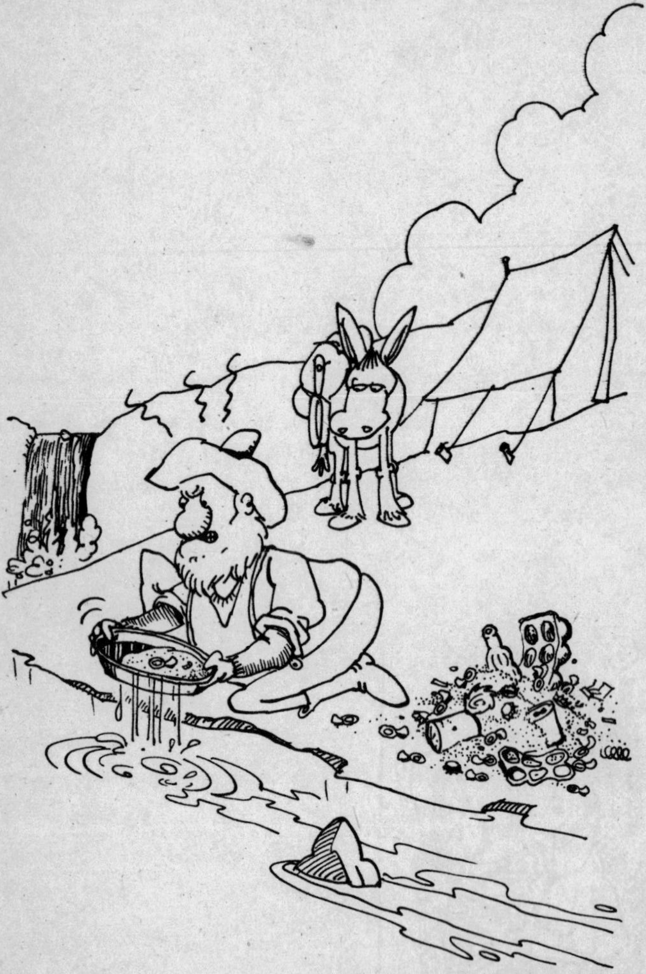

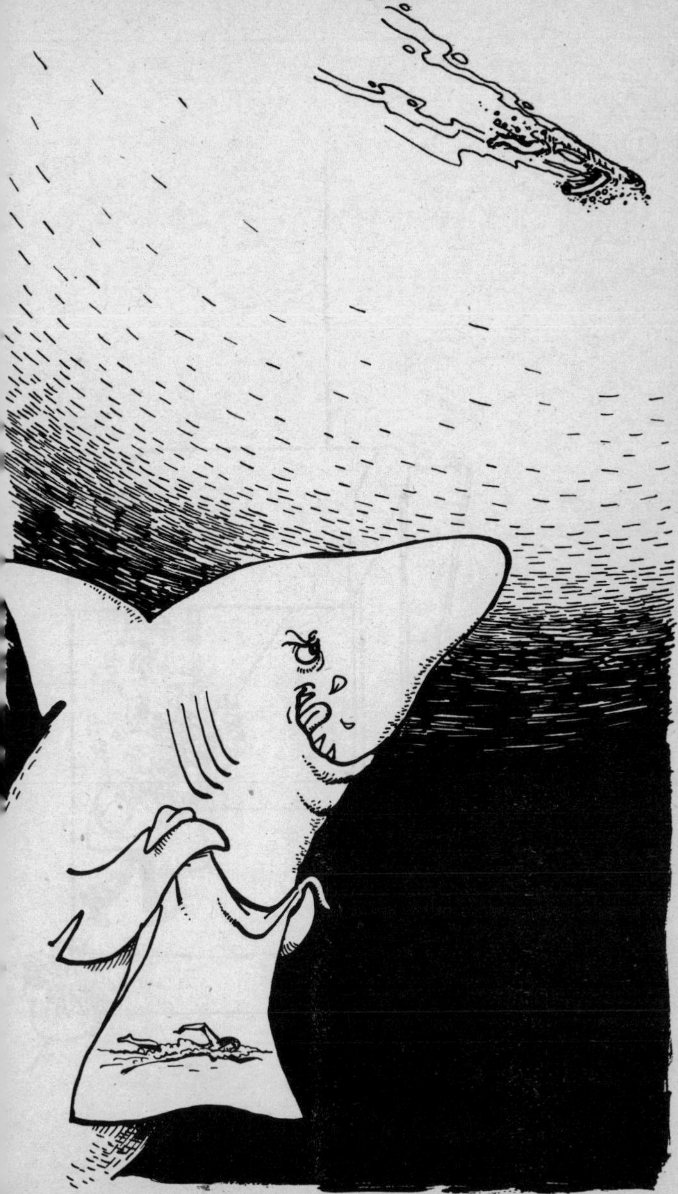

①

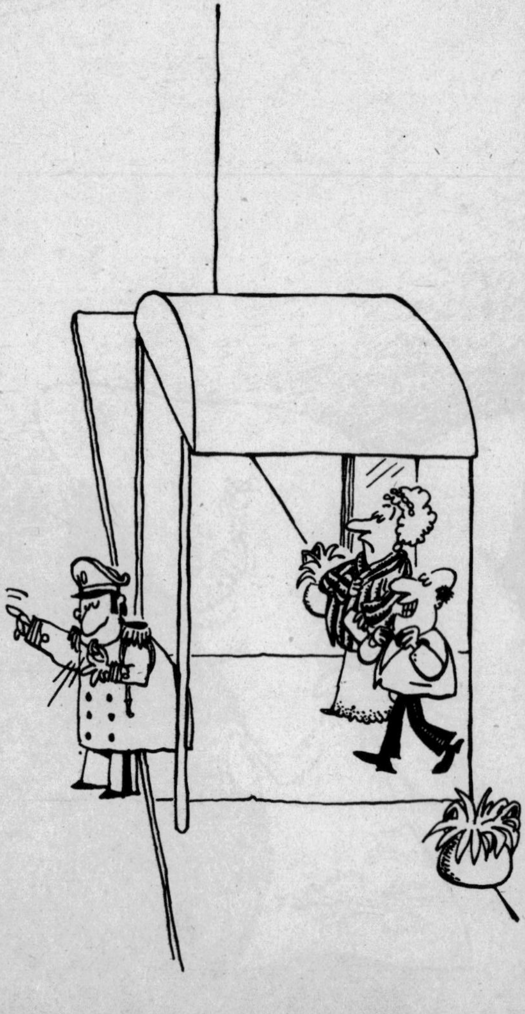

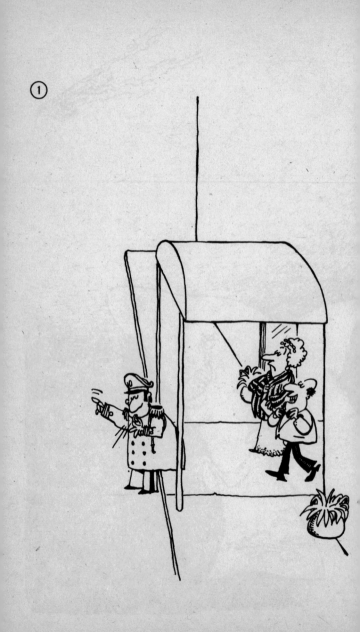

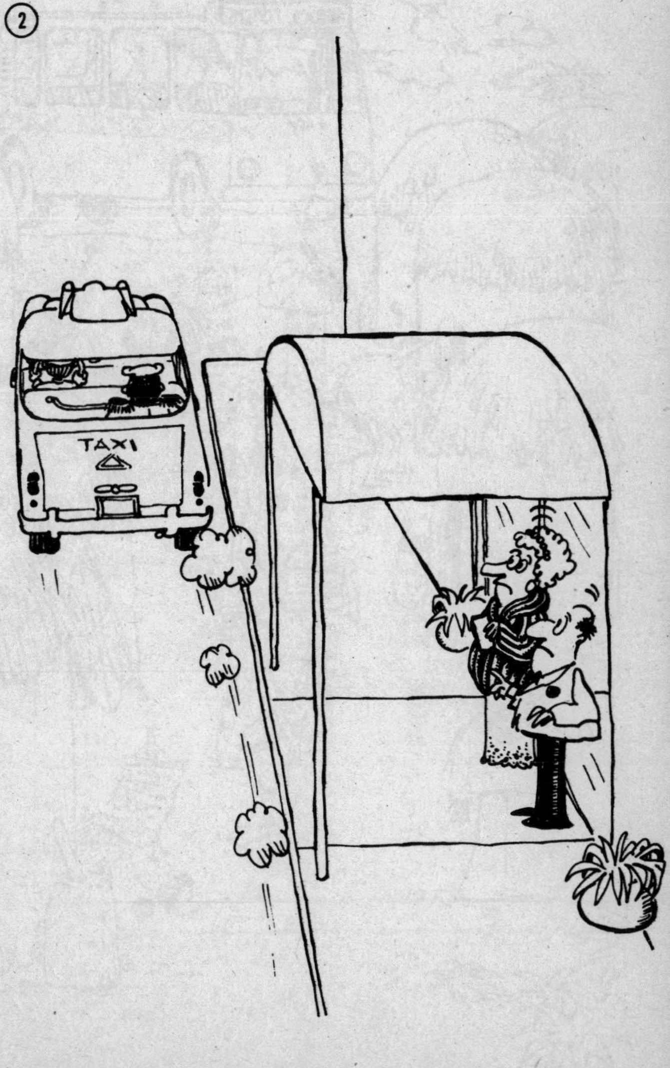
2
TAXI

1

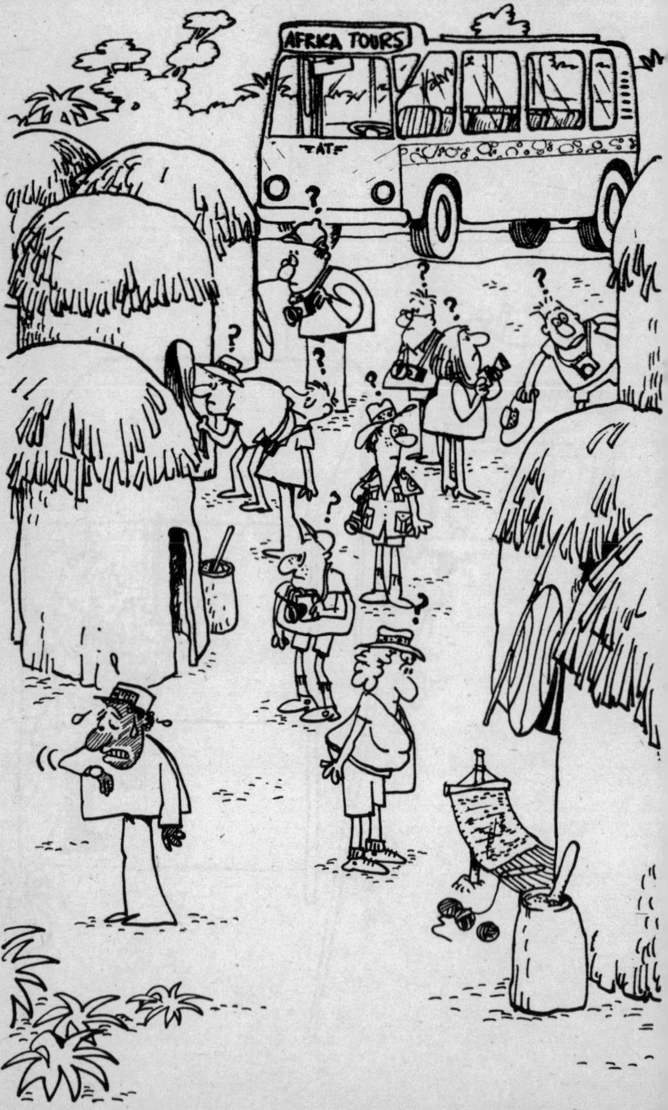
AFRICA TOURS
AT

(2)

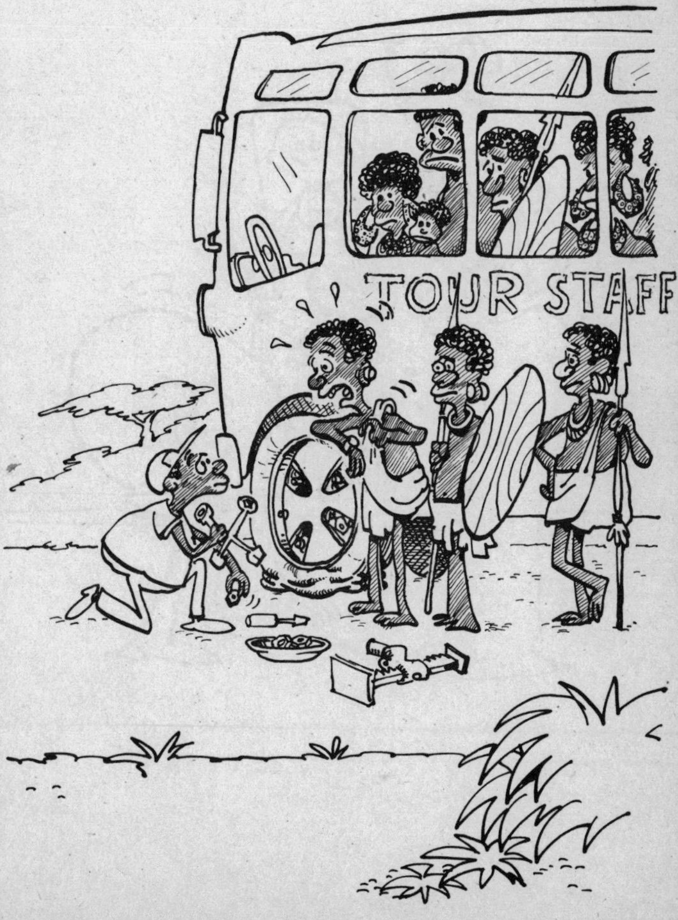
TOUR STAFF

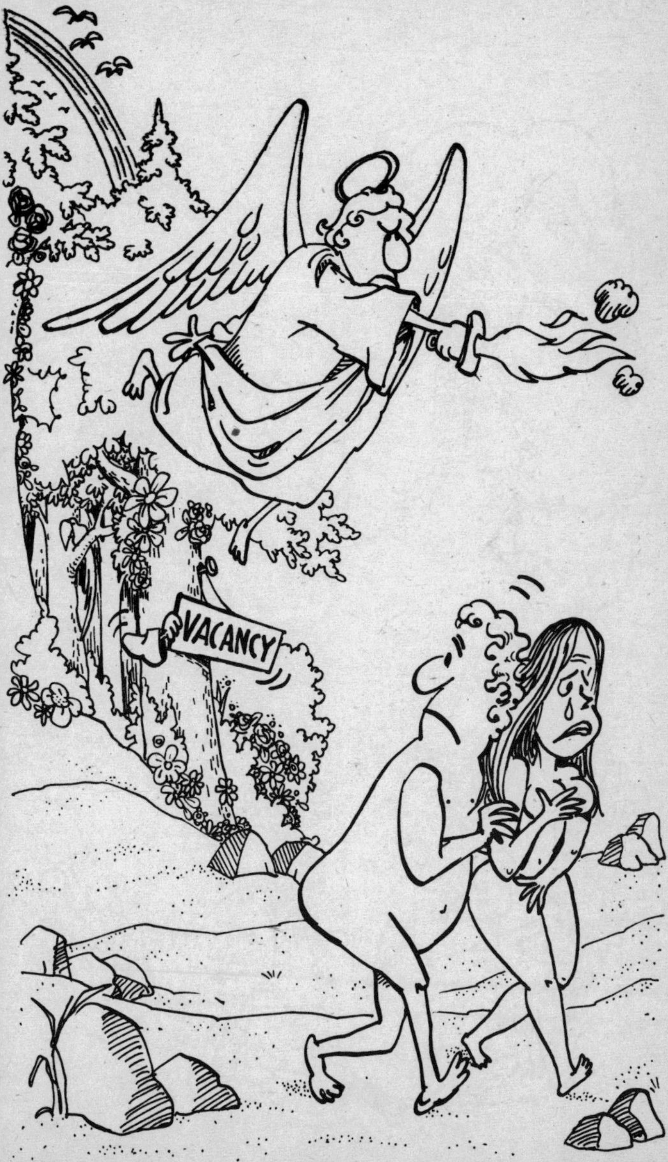
VACANCY

①

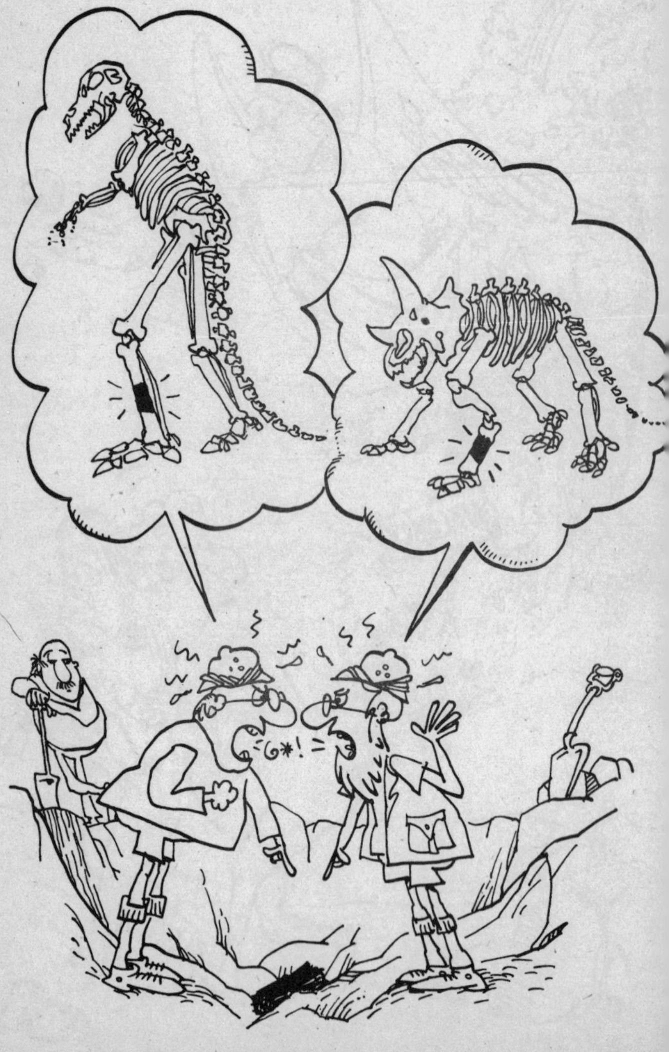

2

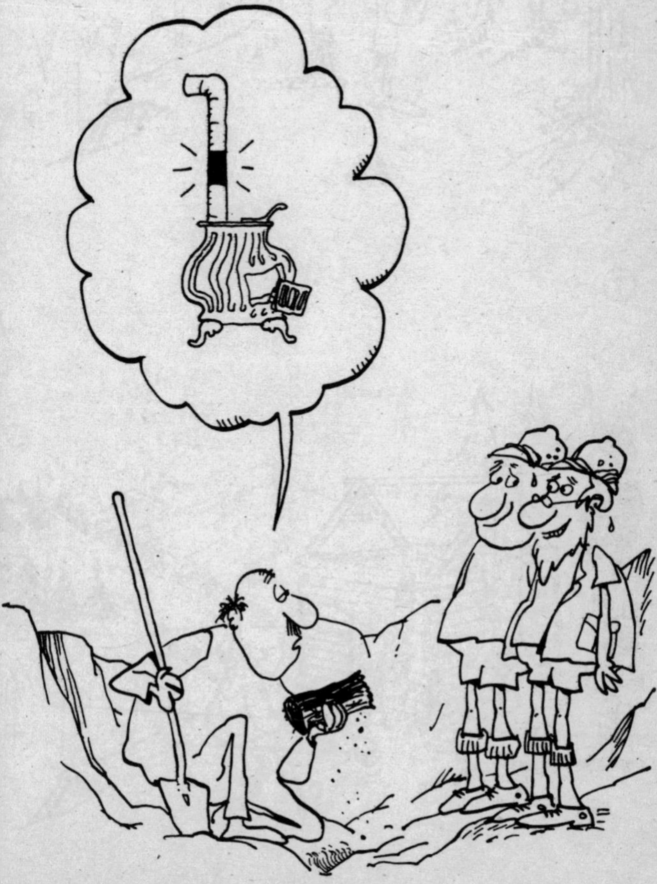

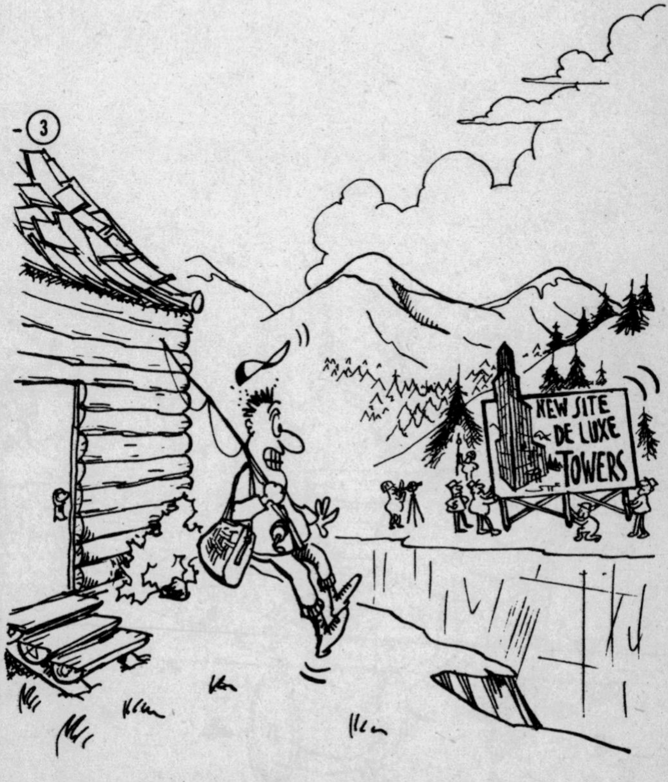
NEW SITE
DE LUXE
TOWERS

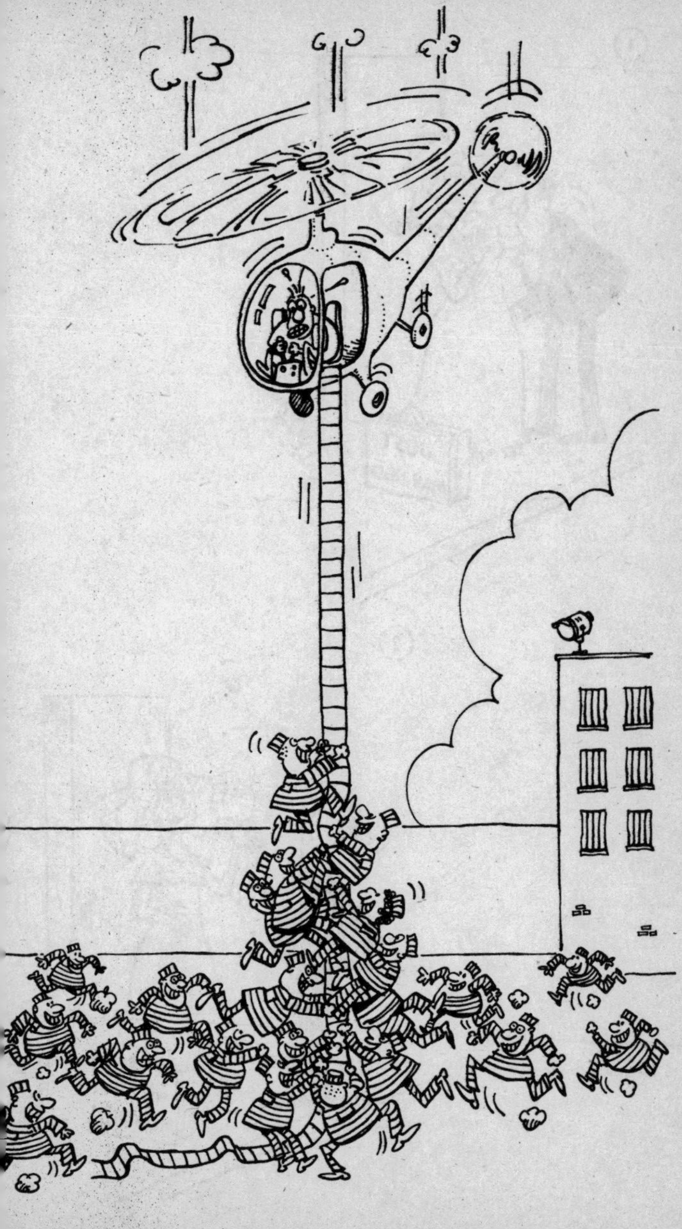

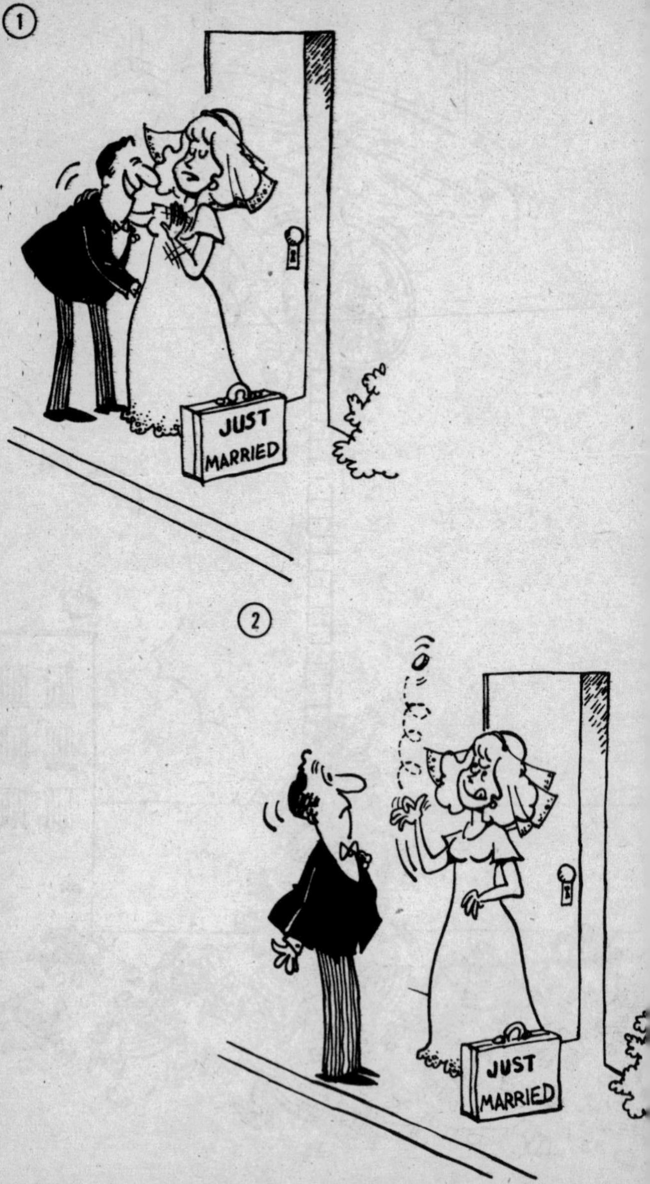
1
JUST MARRIED
2
JUST MARRIED

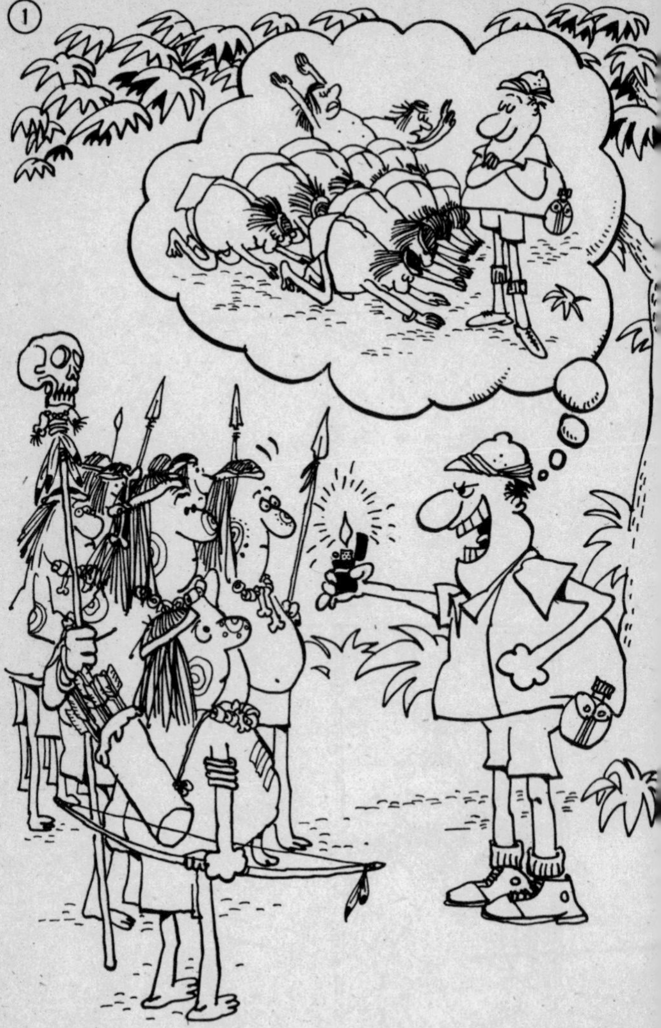

2

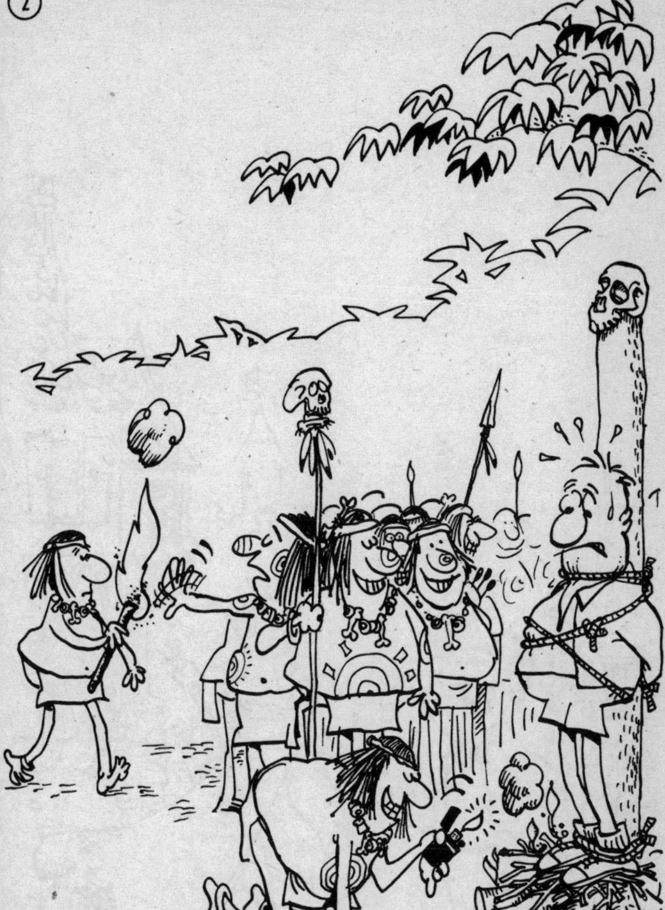

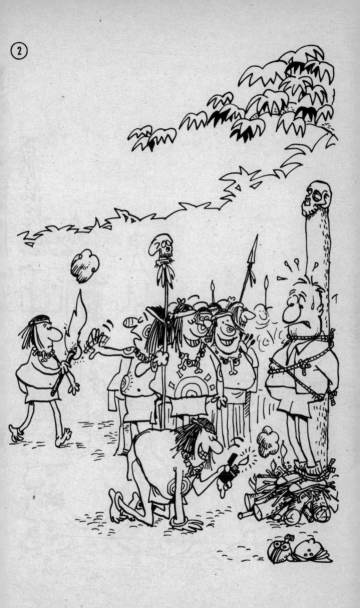

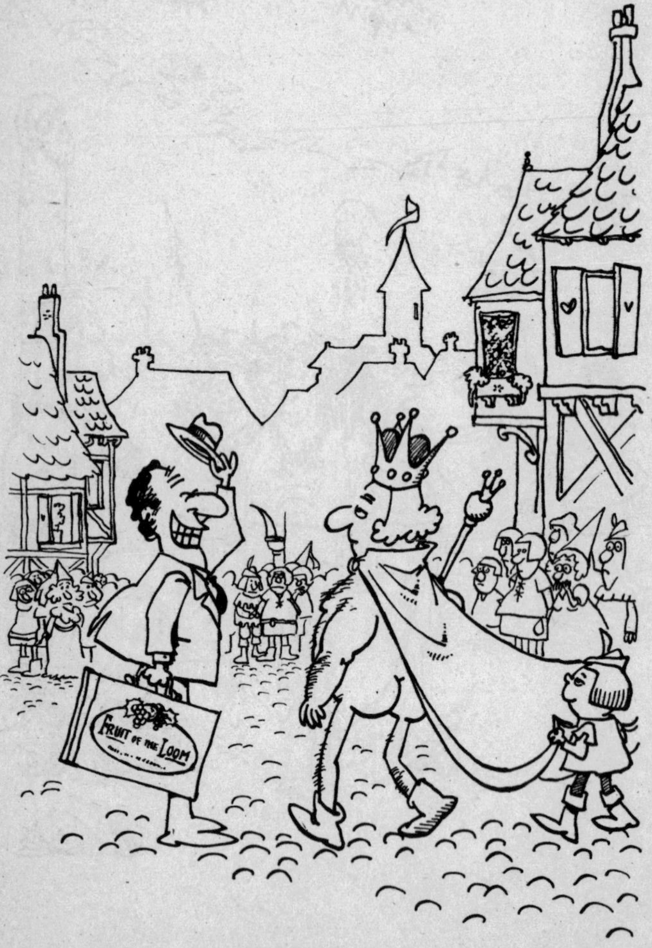
FRUIT OF THE LOOM

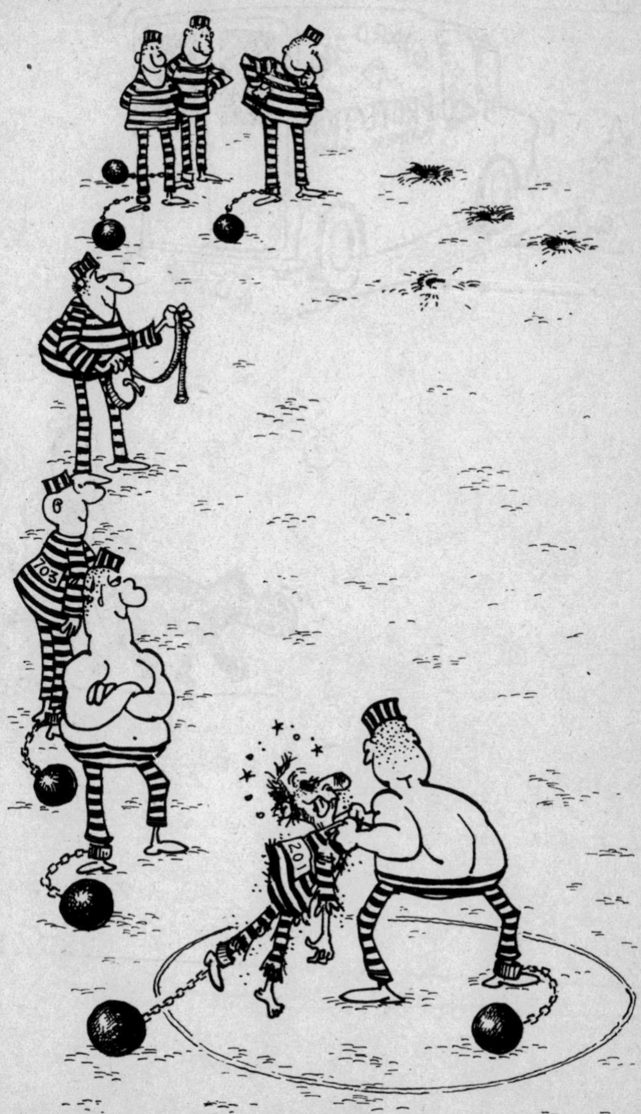
703
201

1

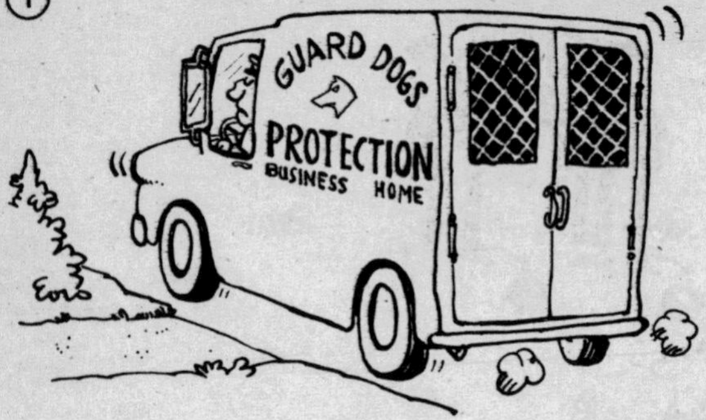
GUARD DOGS
PROTECTION
BUSINESS HOME

2

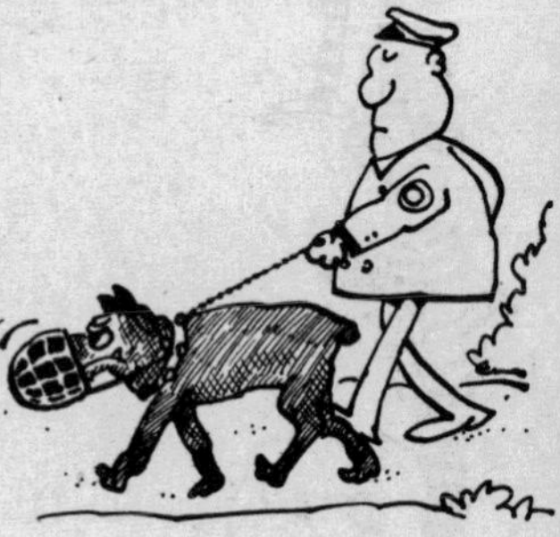

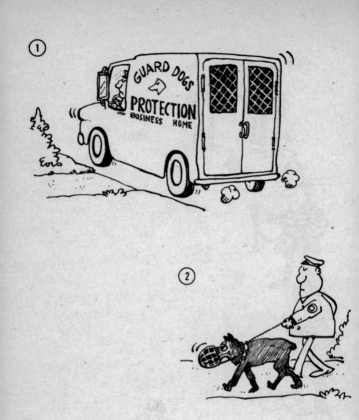

3

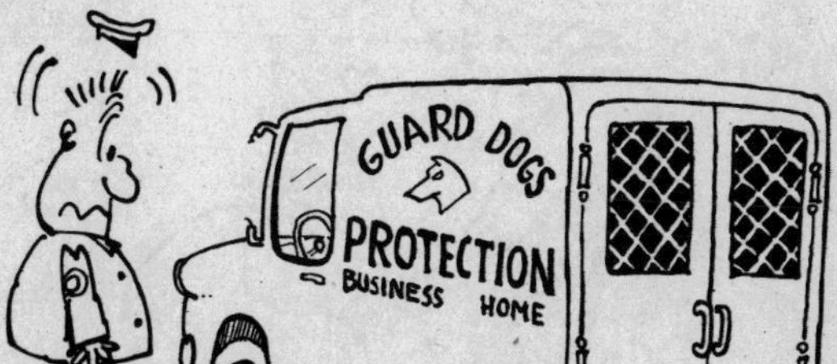
GUARD DOGS
PROTECTION
BUSINESS HOME

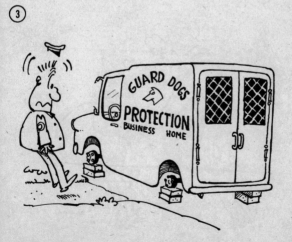

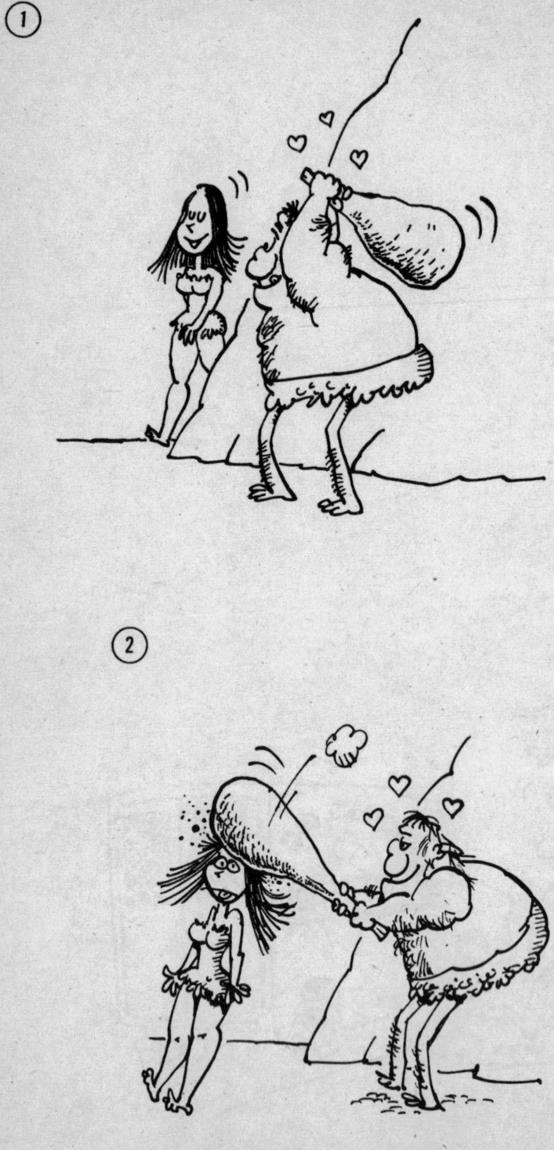

3

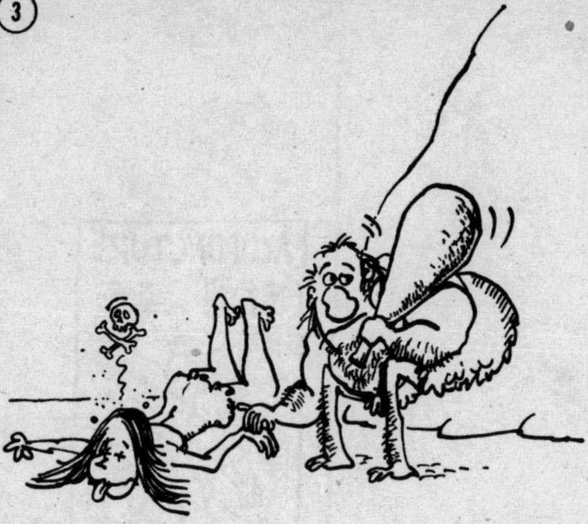

4

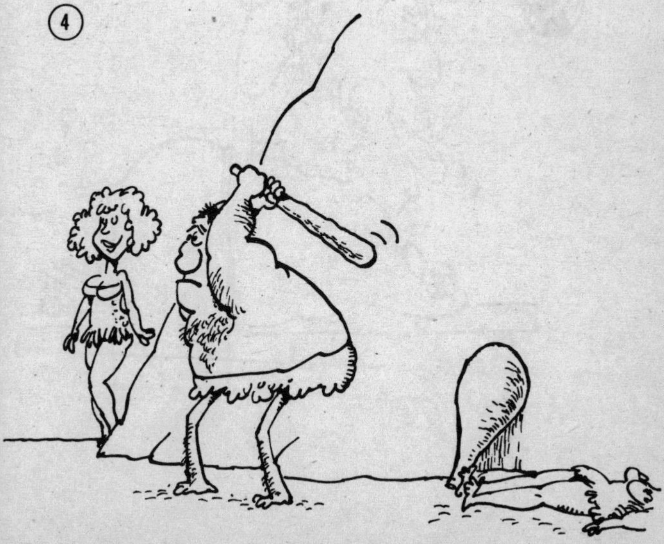

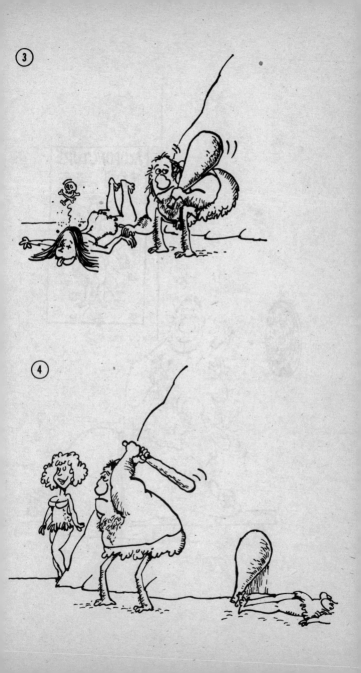

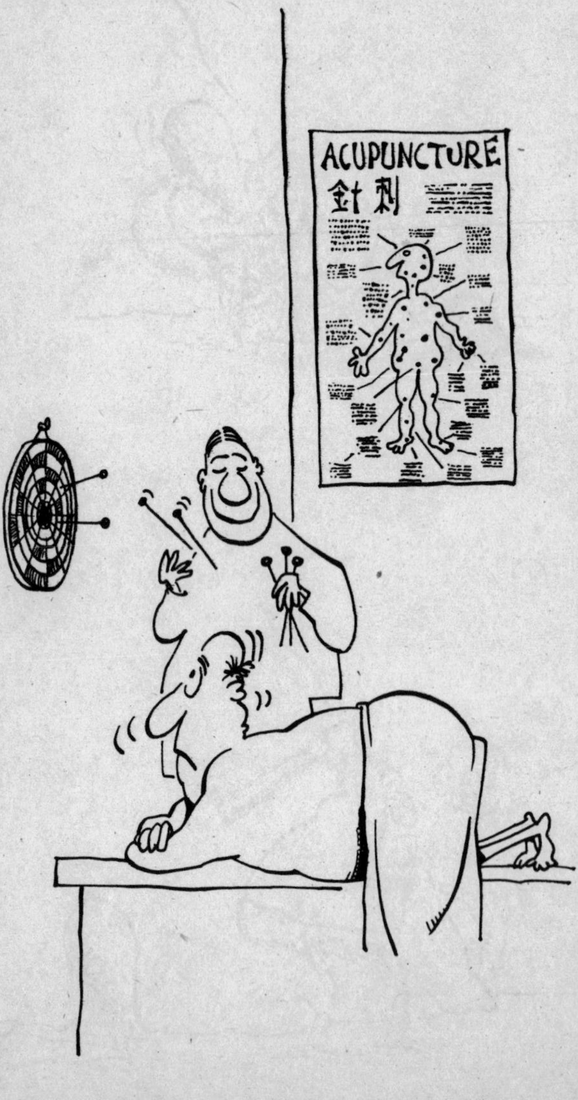
ACUPUNCTURE
針刺

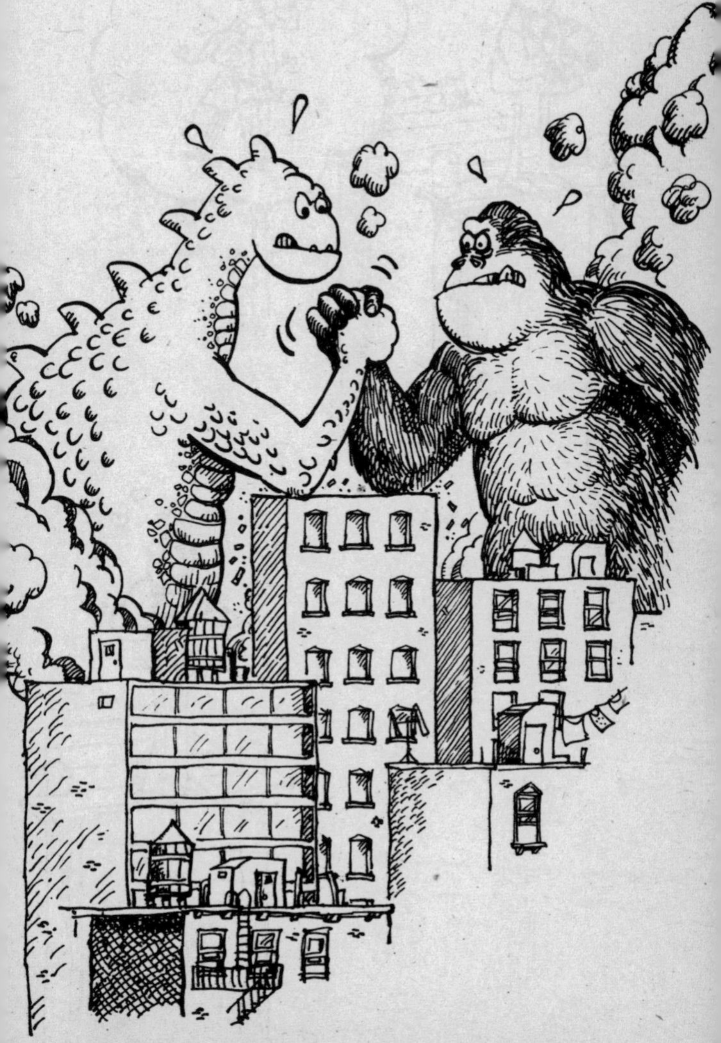

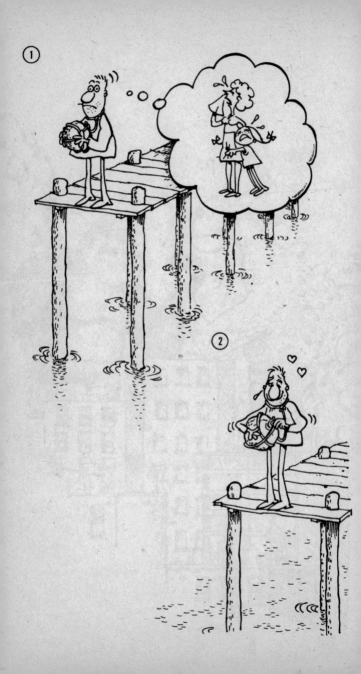

1

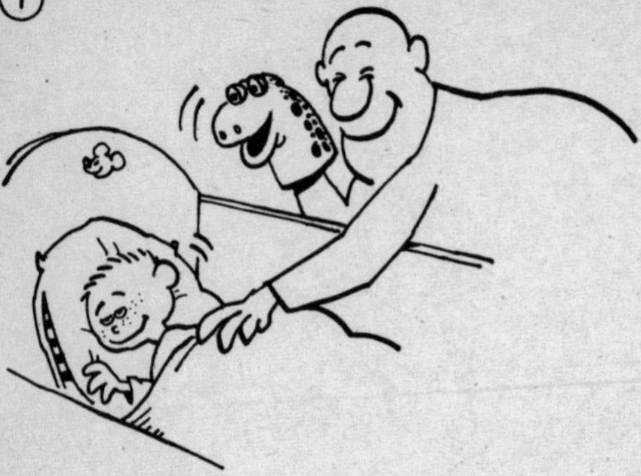

2

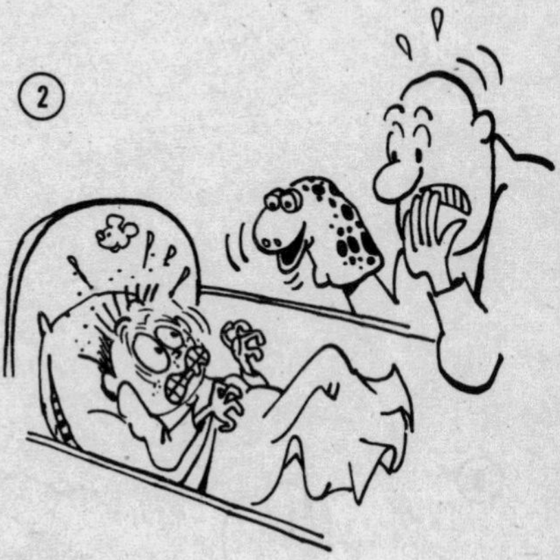

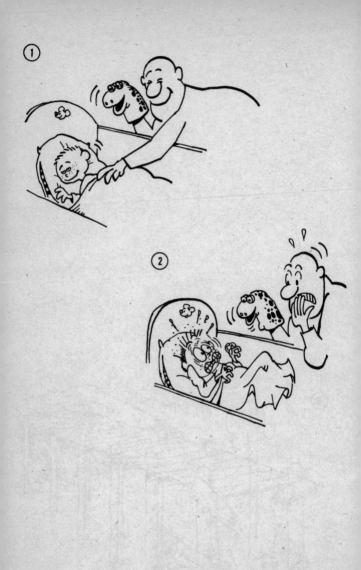

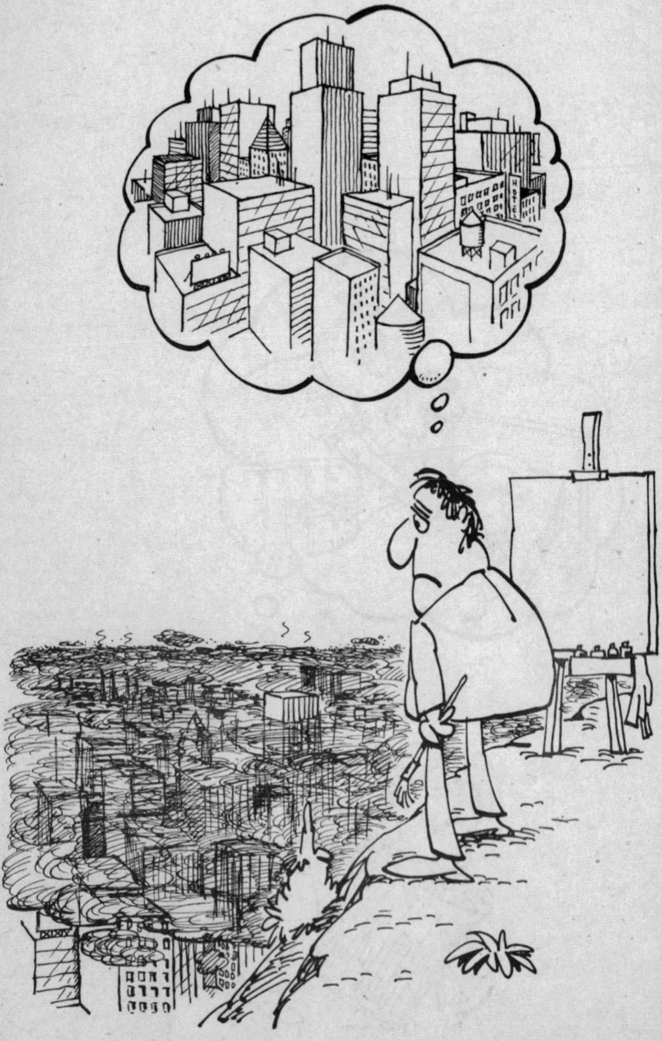

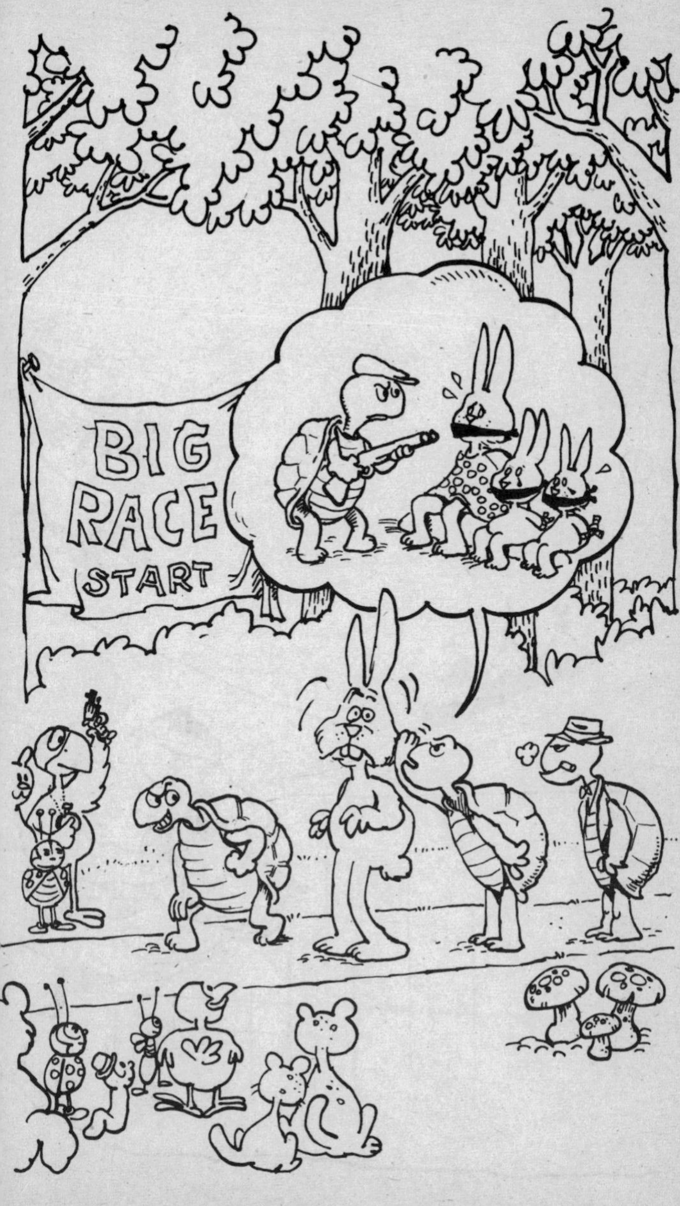
BIG RACE
START

①

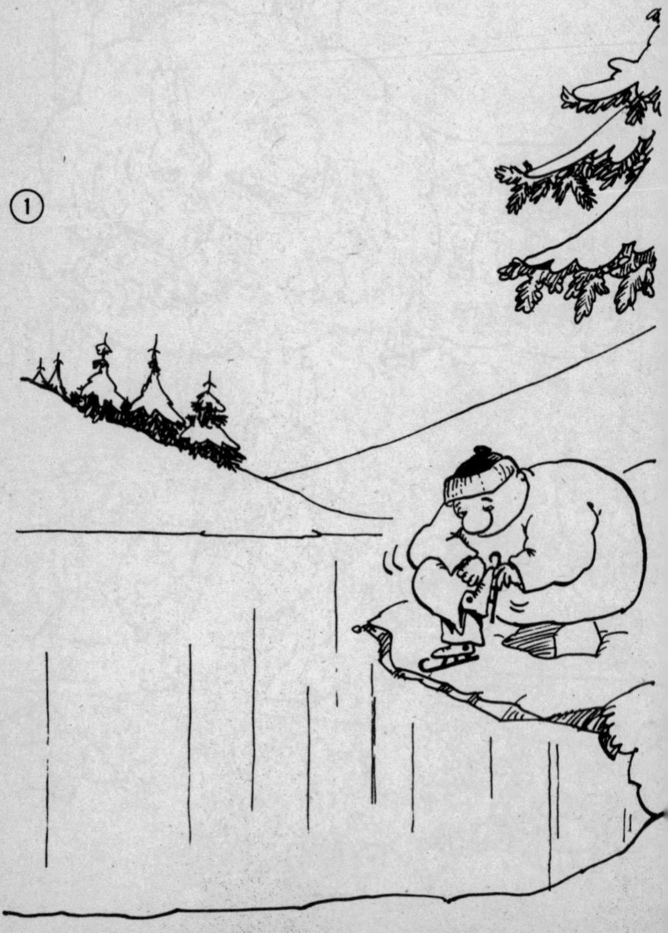

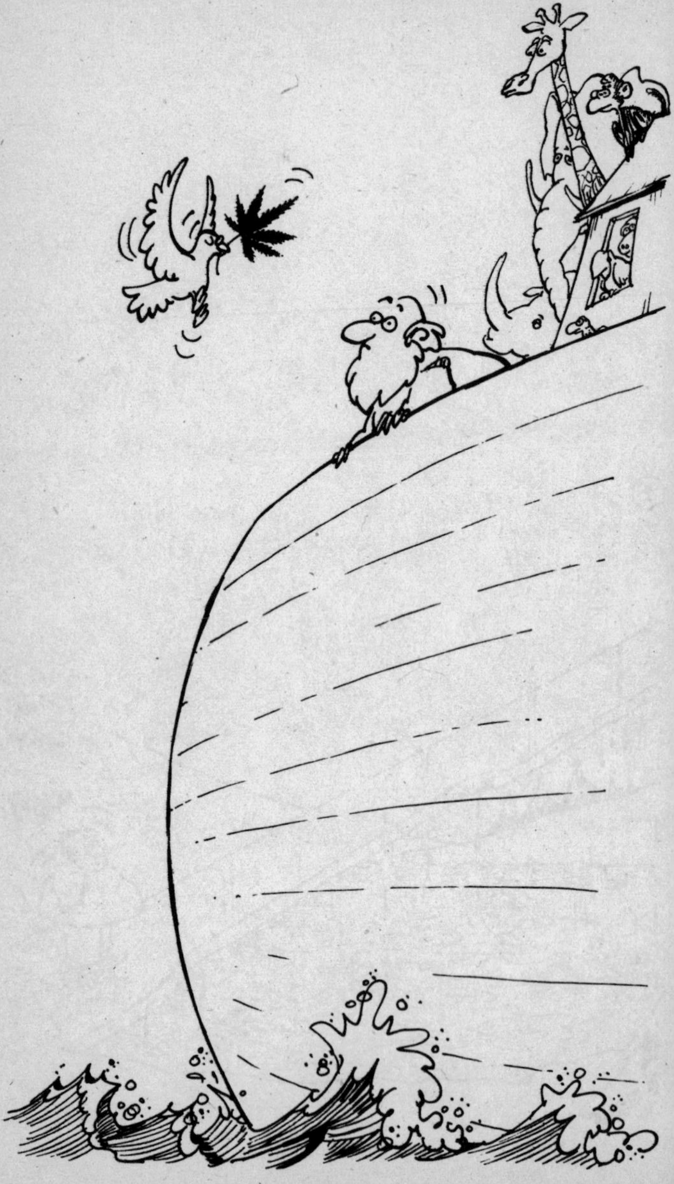

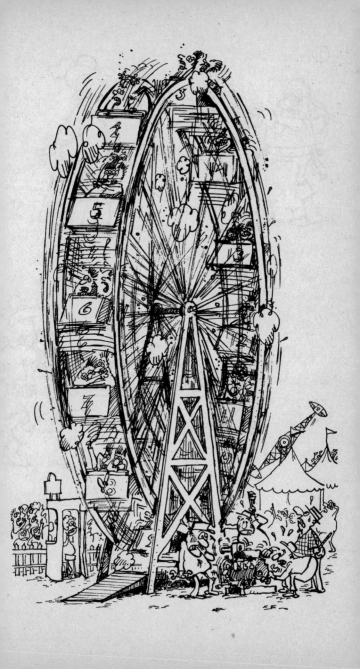

1

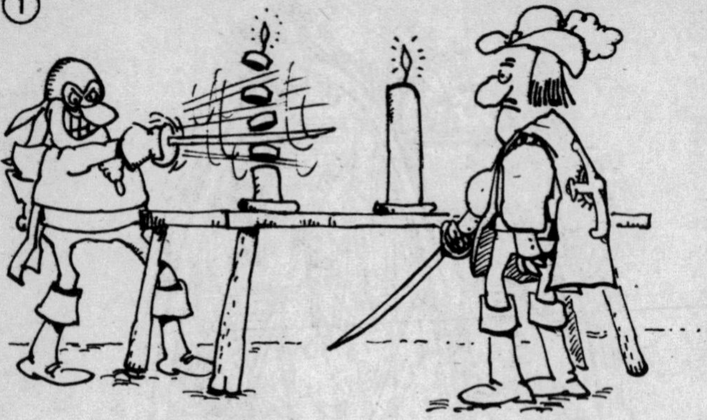

2

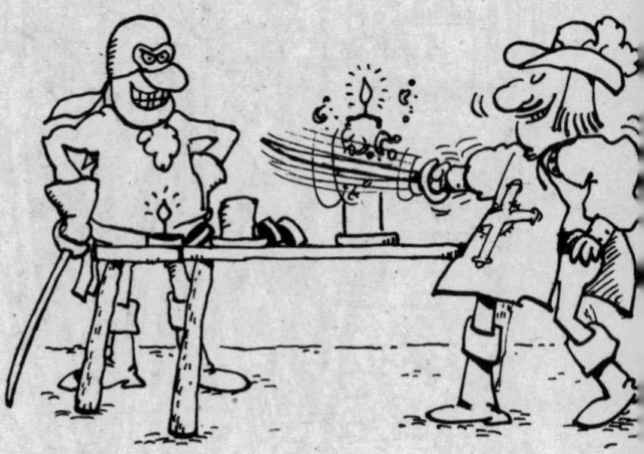

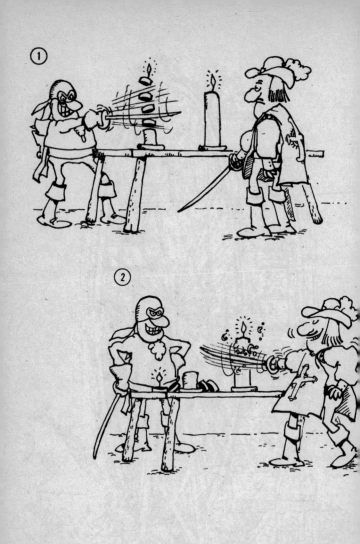

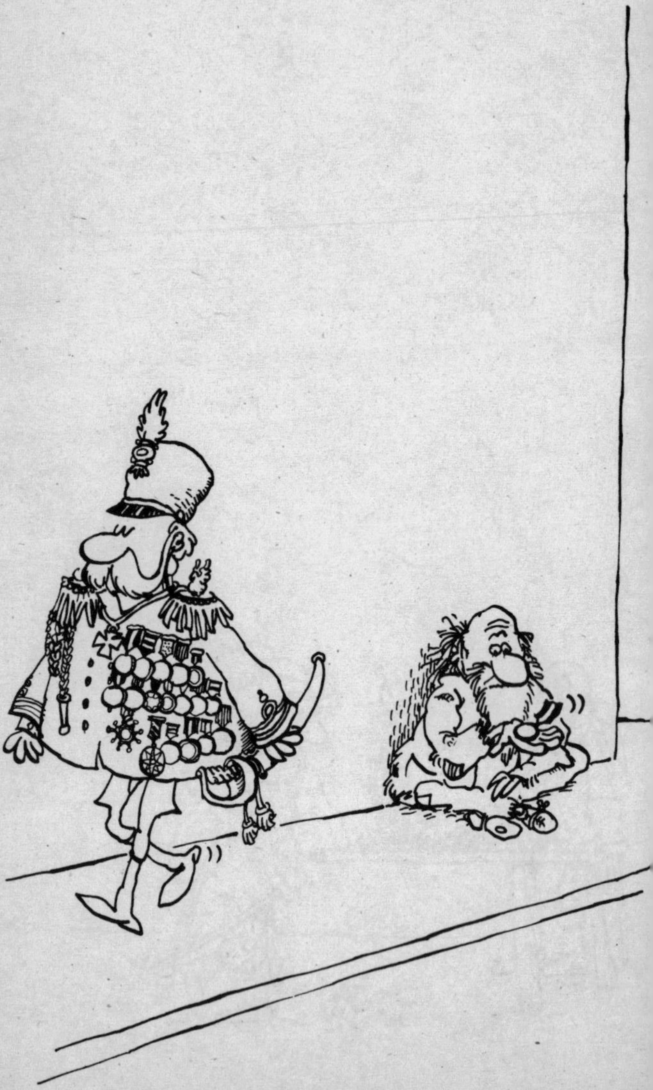

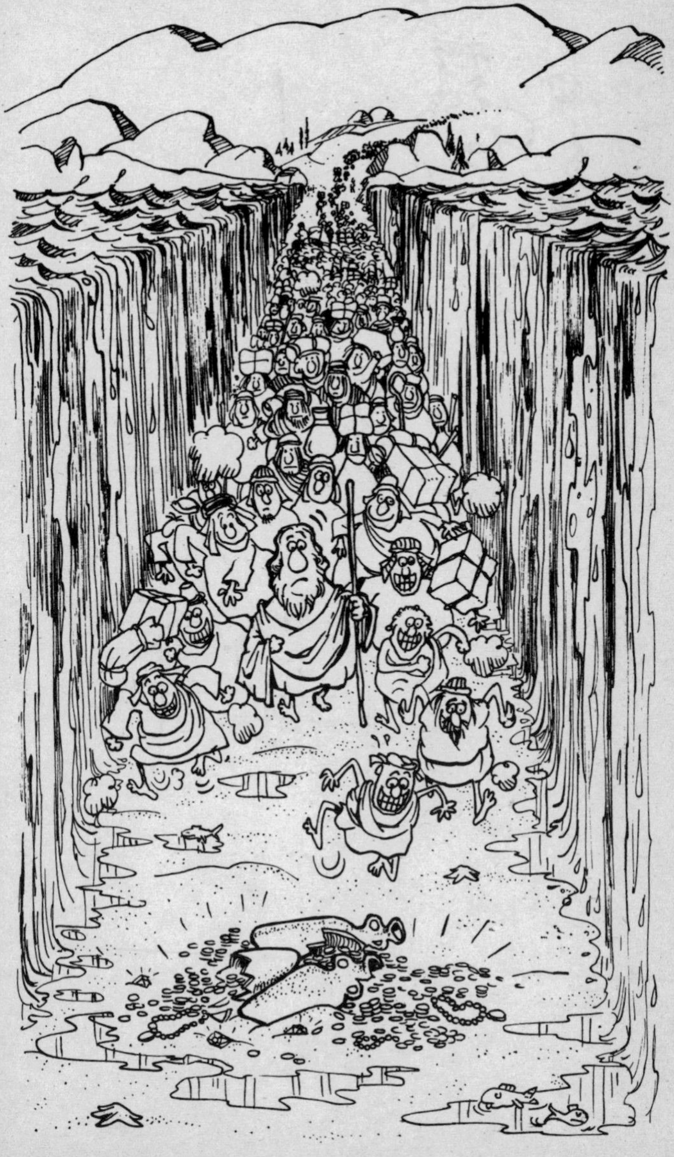

①

②

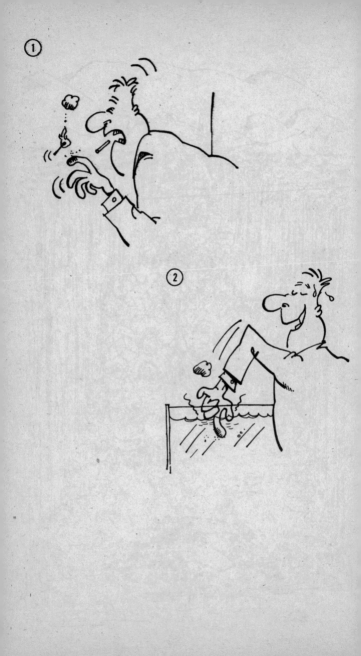

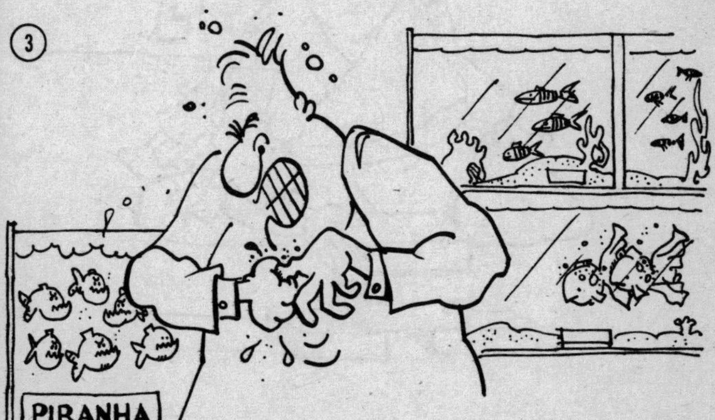
3
PIRANHA

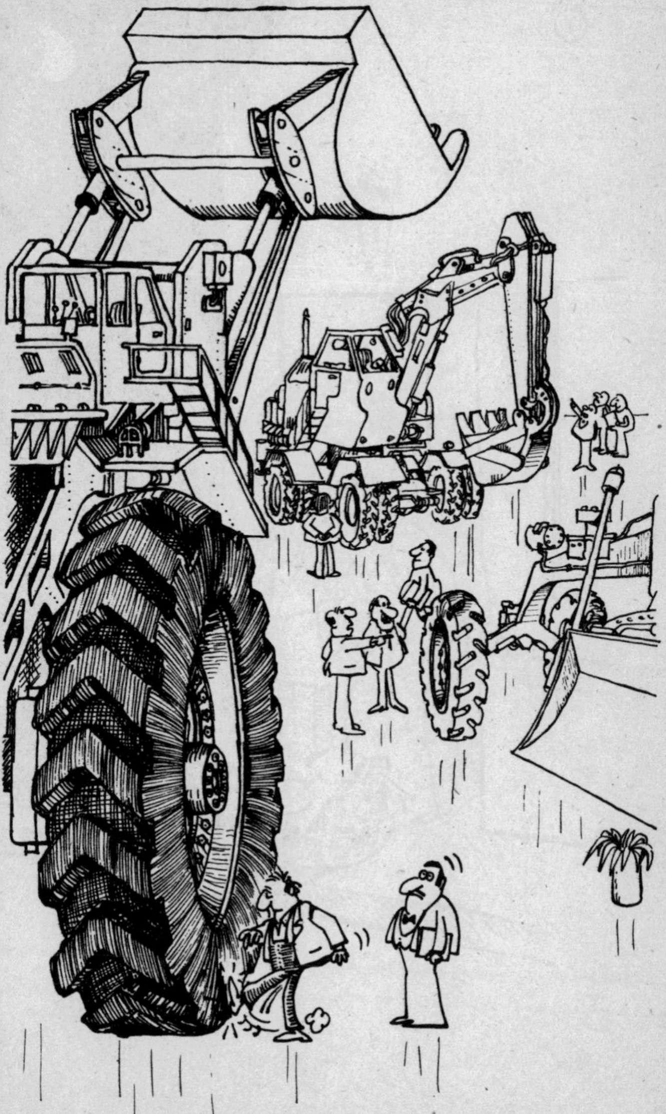

1

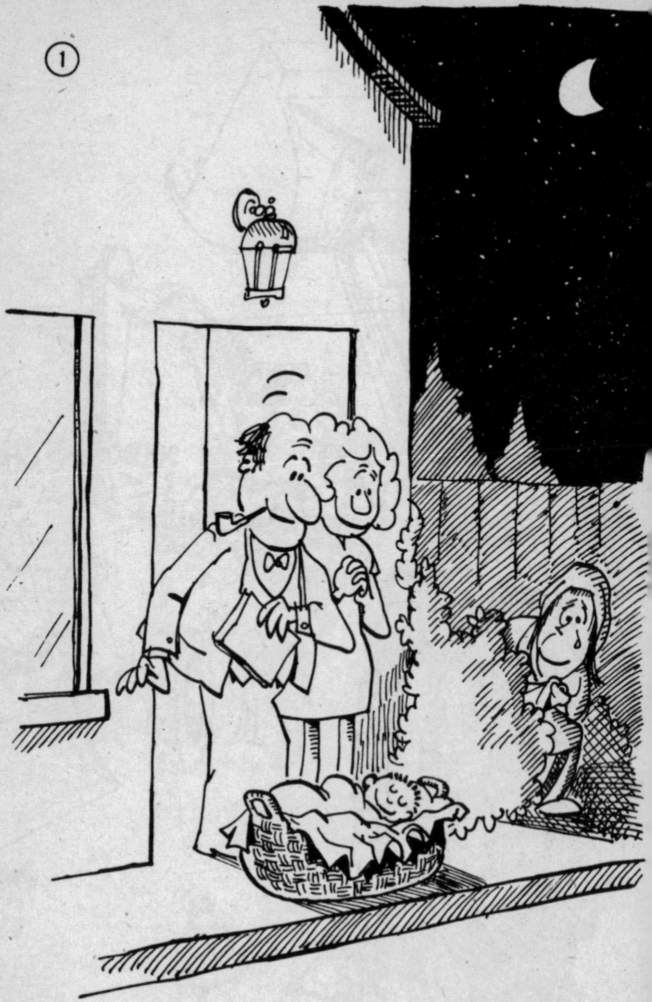

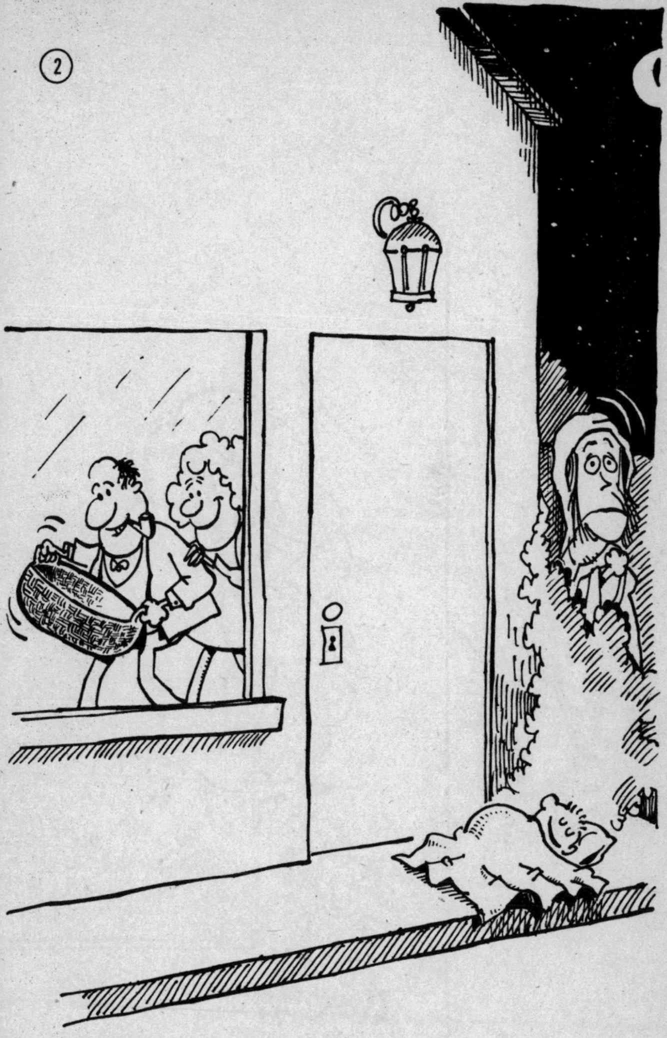

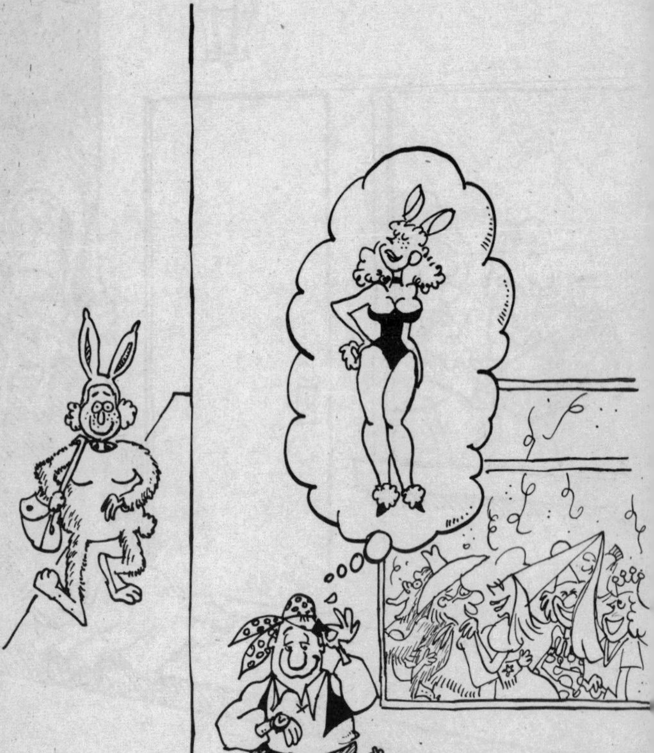

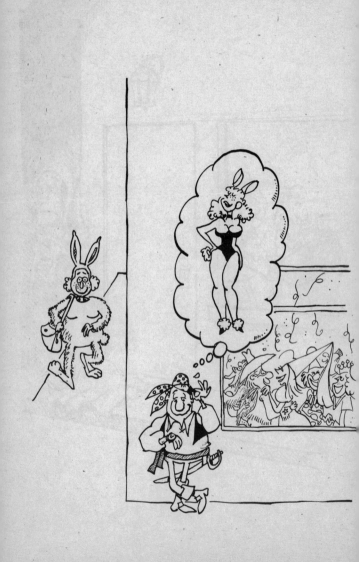

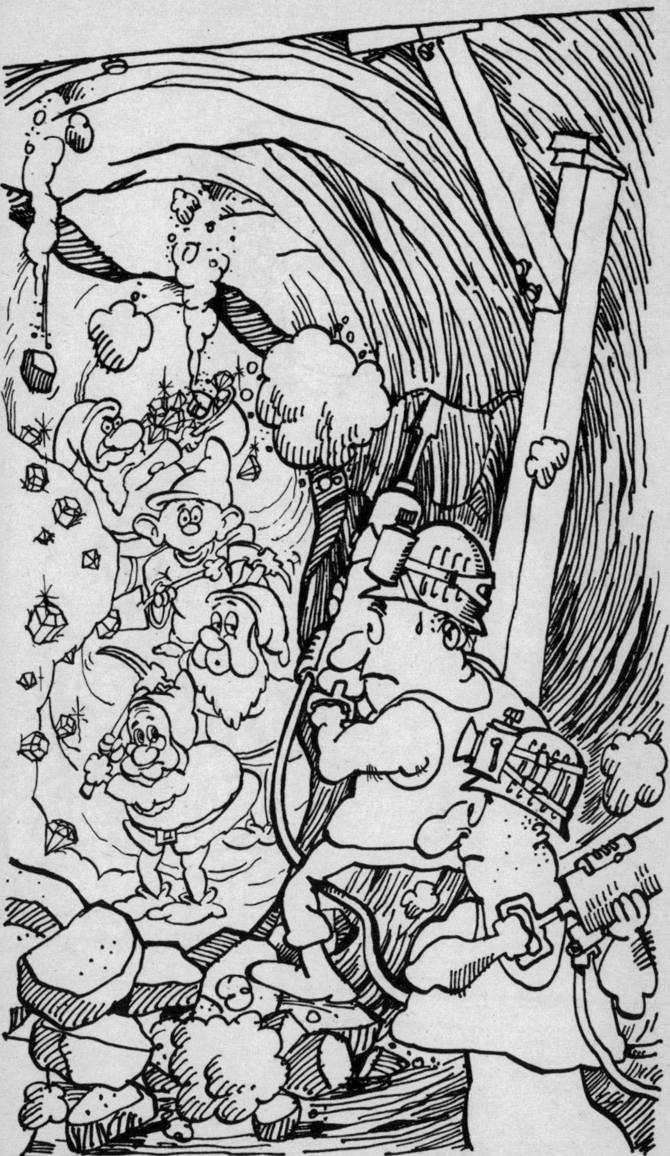

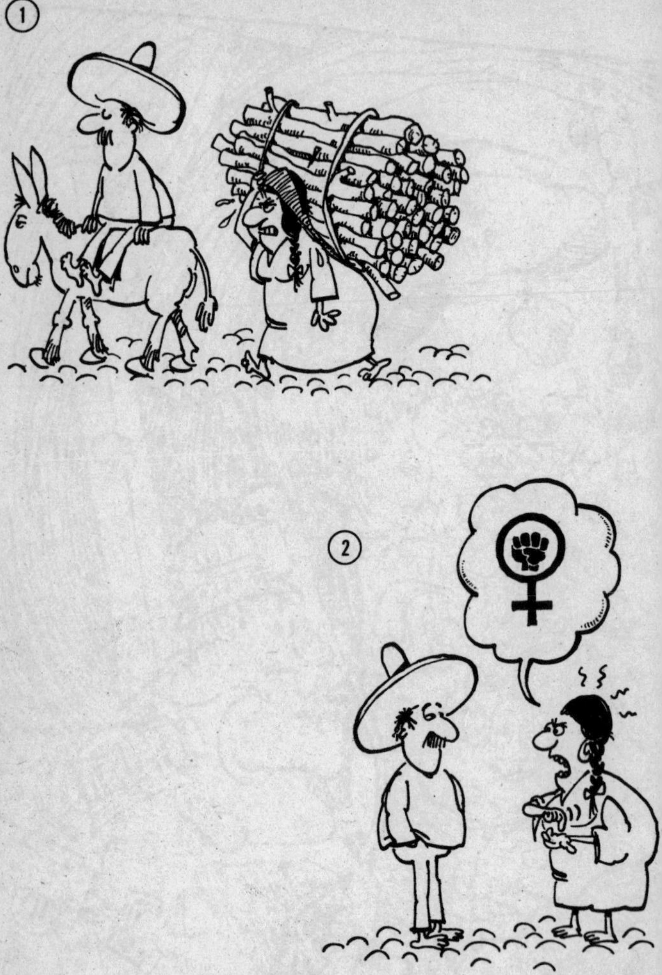
1
2

③

①

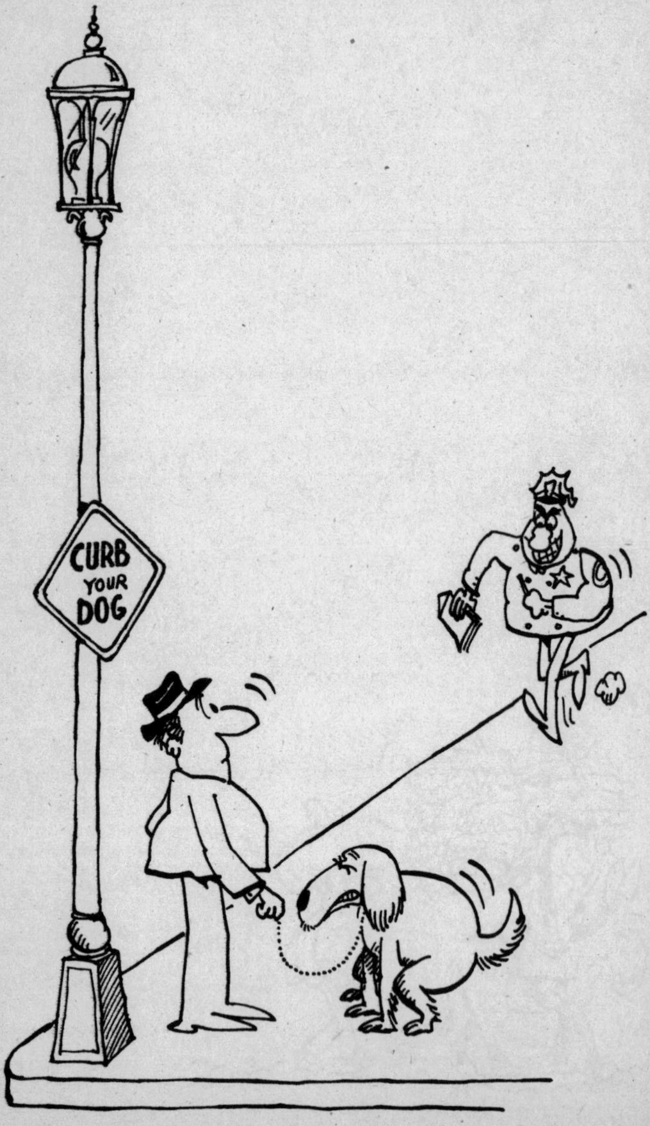
CURB
YOUR
DOG

(2)

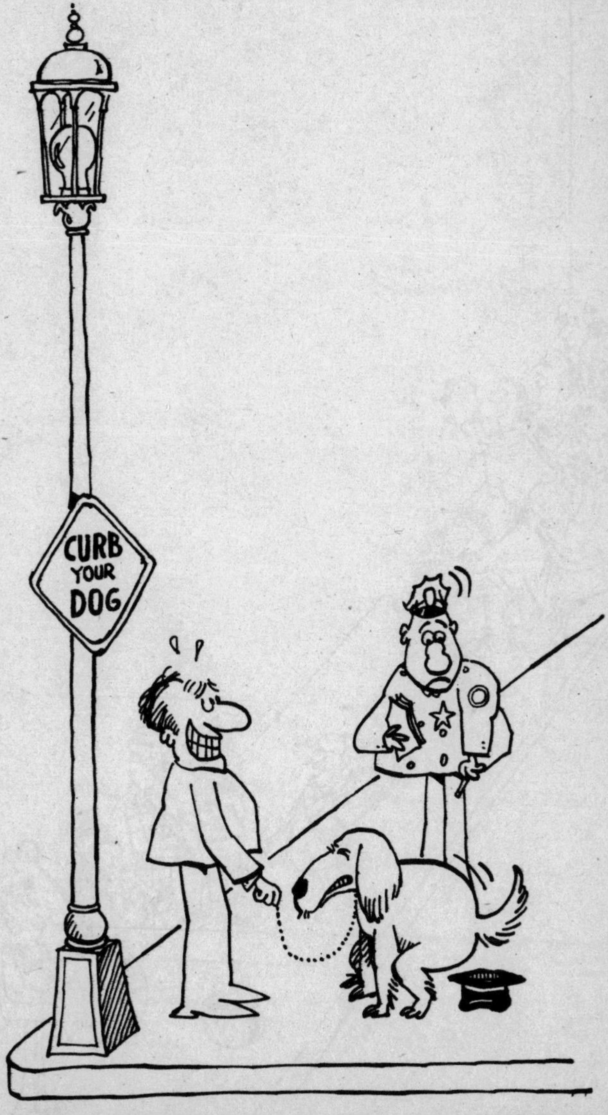
CURB
YOUR
DOG

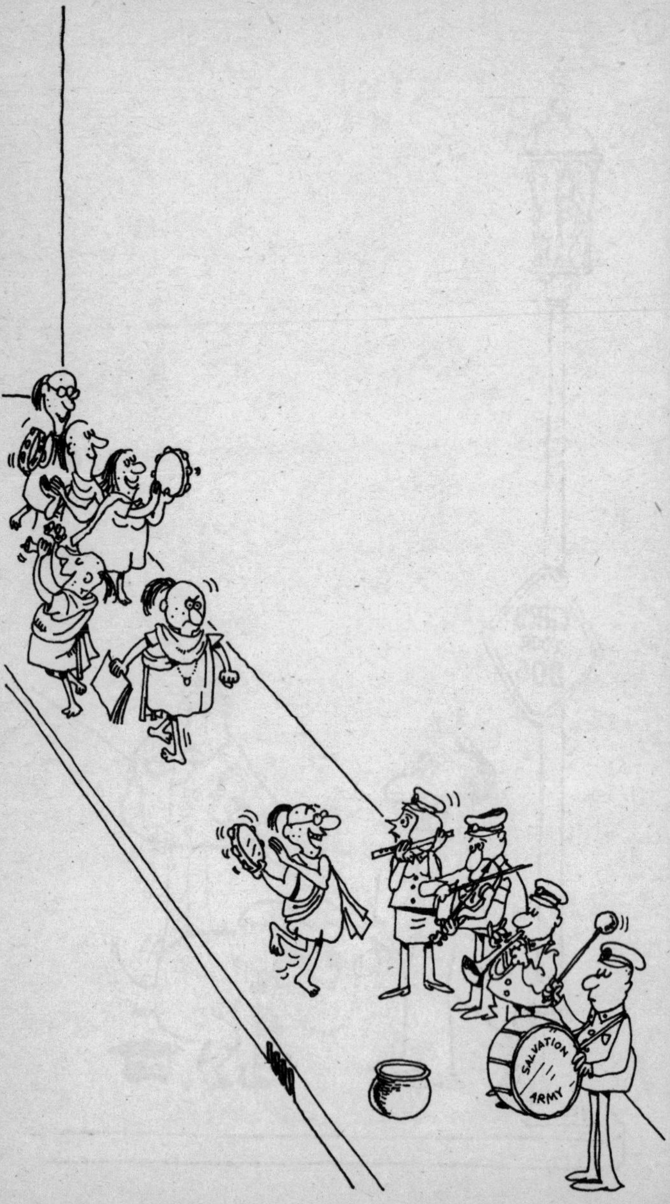
SALVATION ARMY

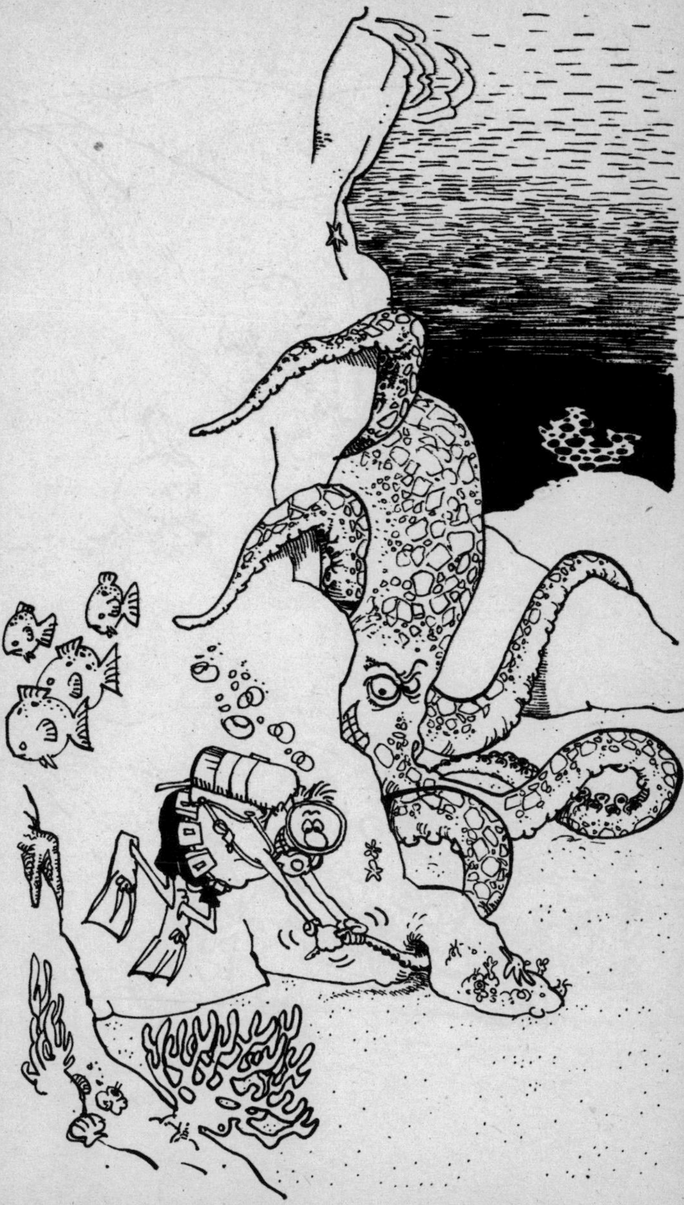

①

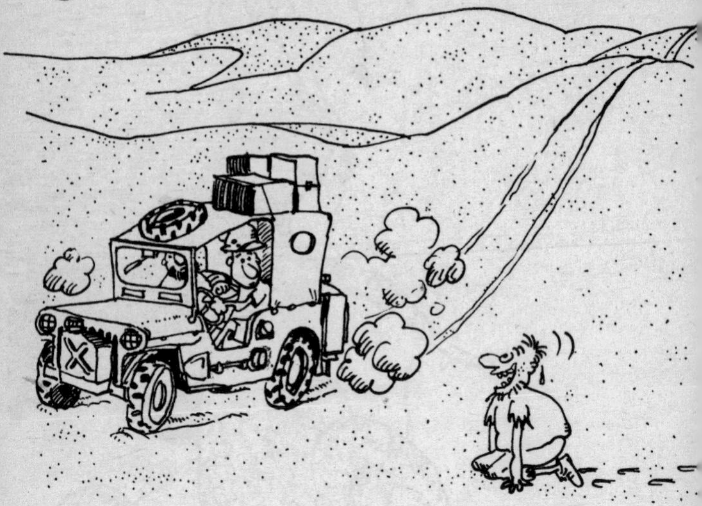

②

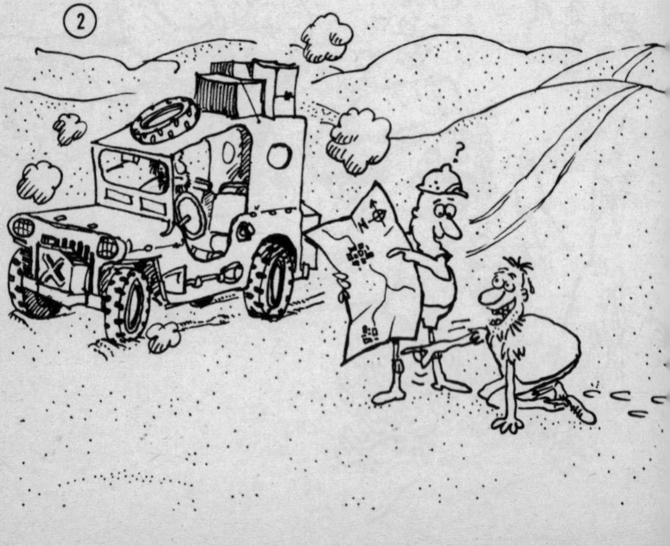

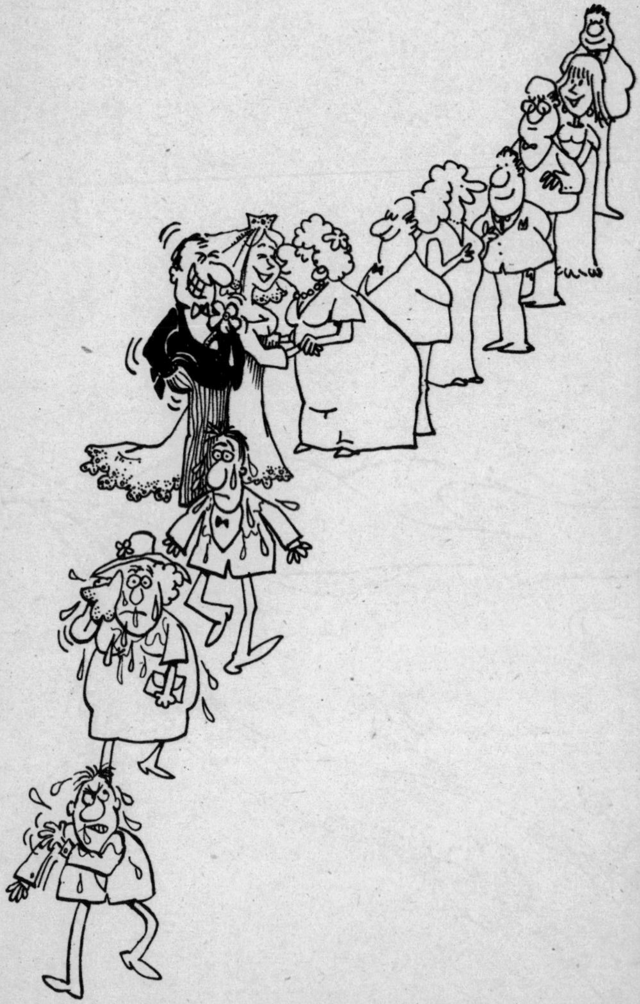

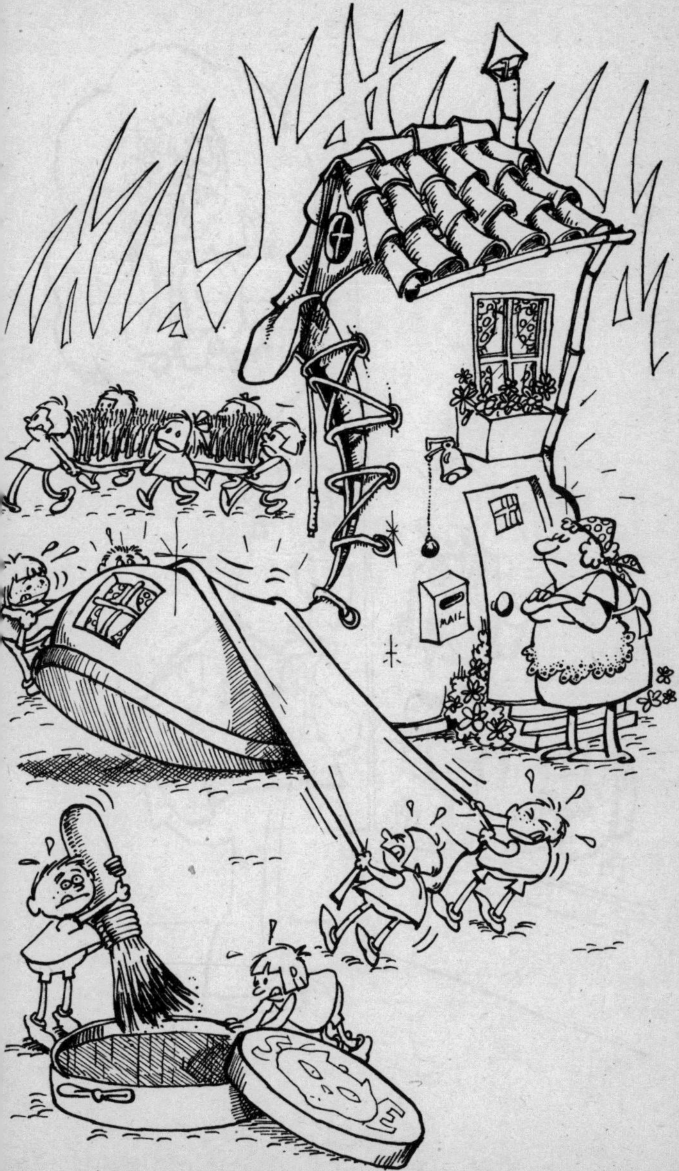
MAIL

(1)

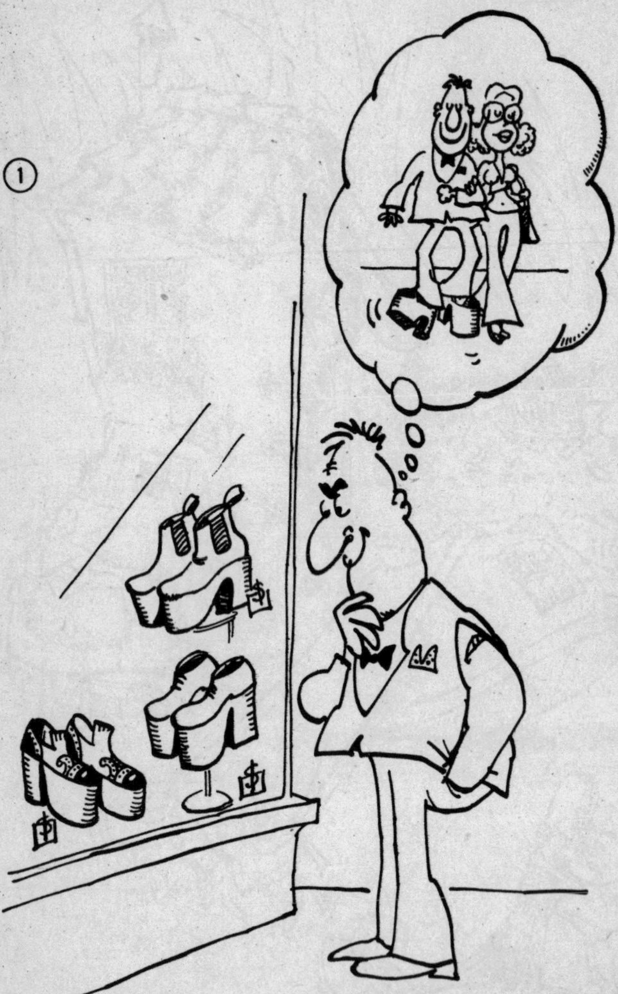

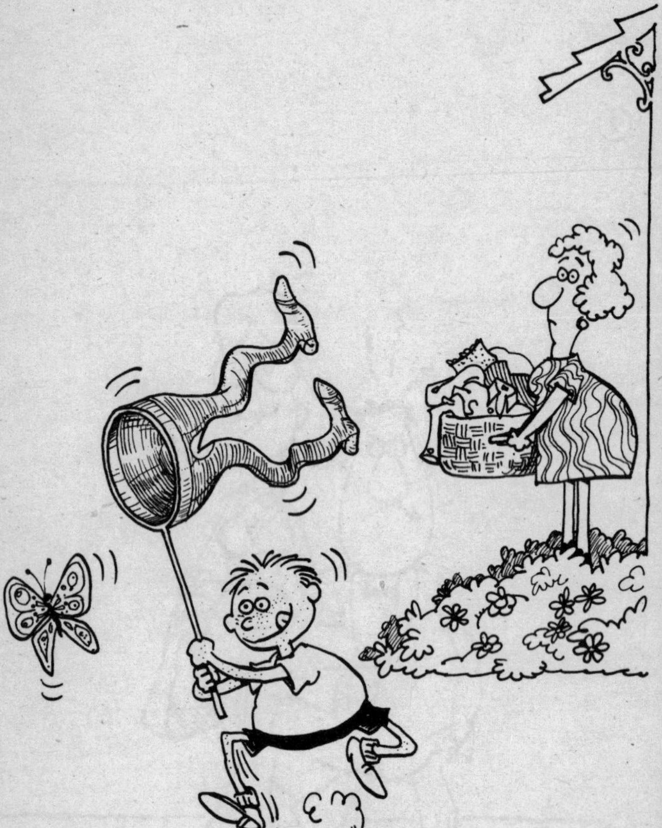

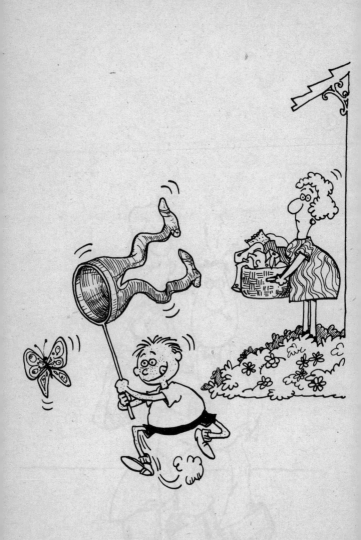

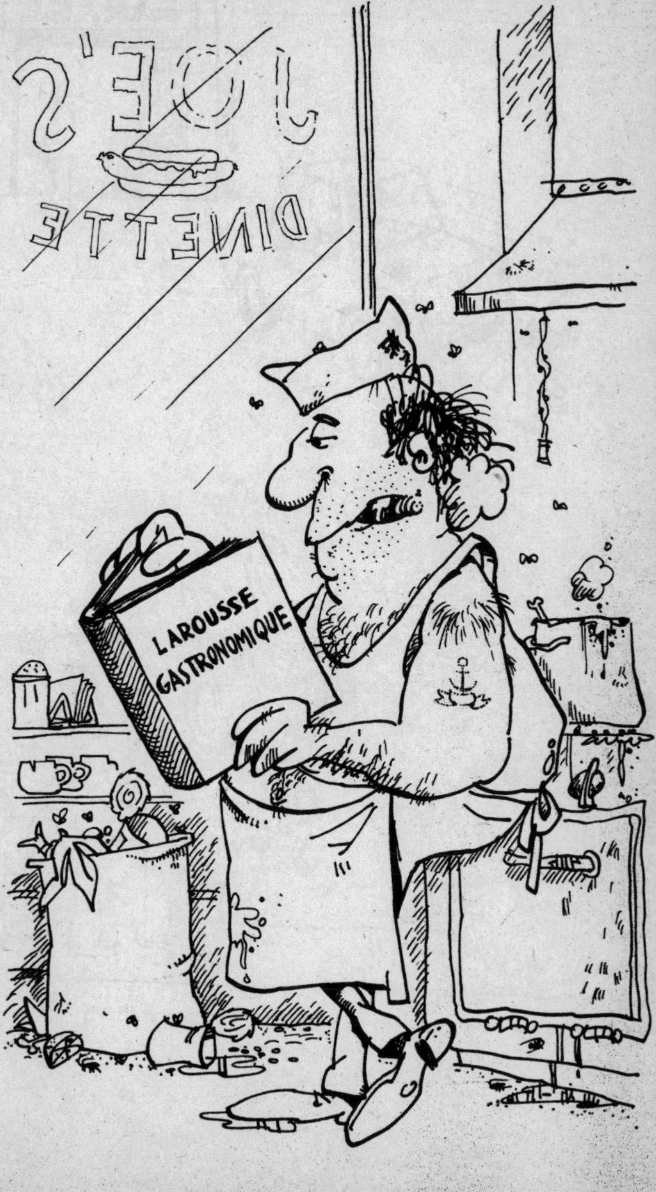
JOE'S
DINETTE
LAROUSSE
GASTRONOMIQUE

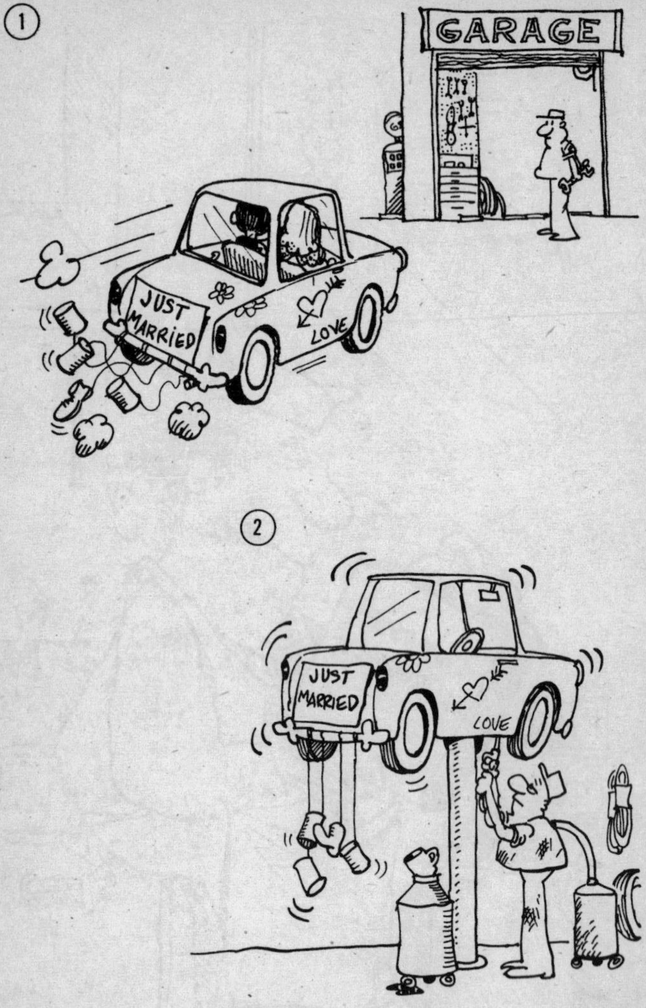
1
GARAGE
JUST MARRIED
LOVE
2
JUST MARRIED
LOVE

3

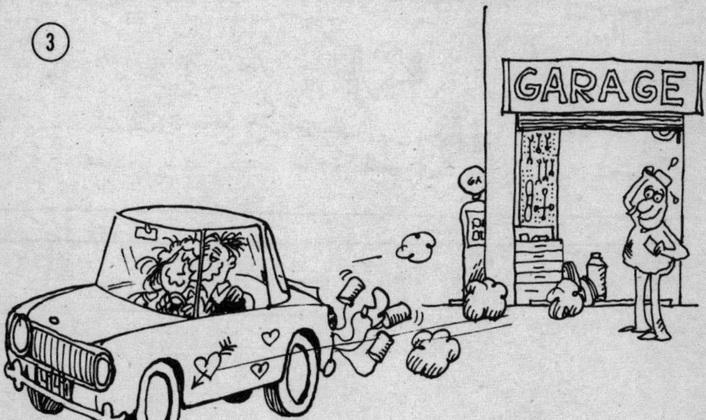
GARAGE

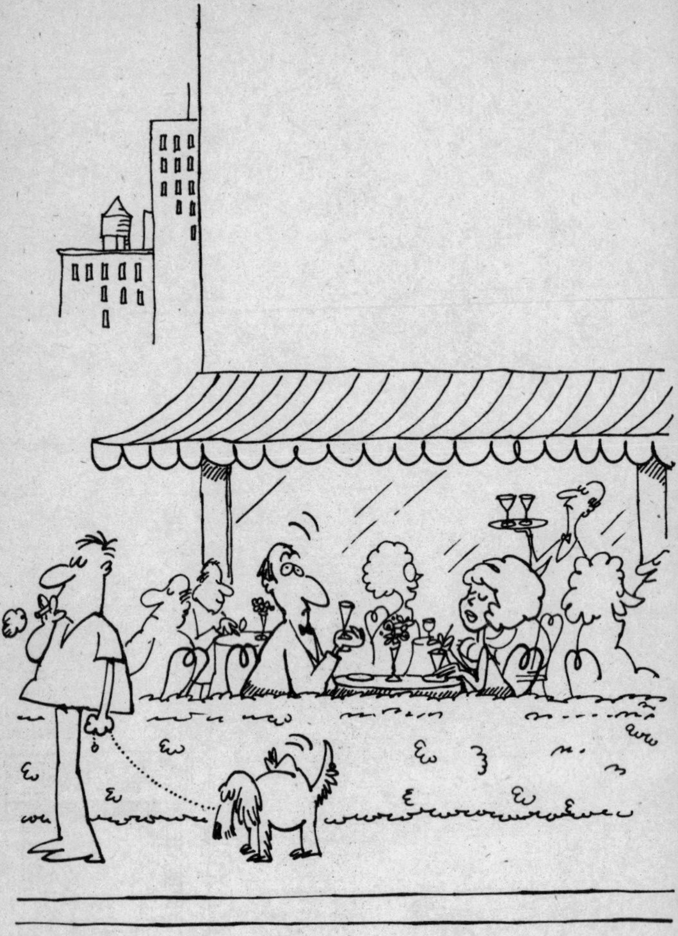

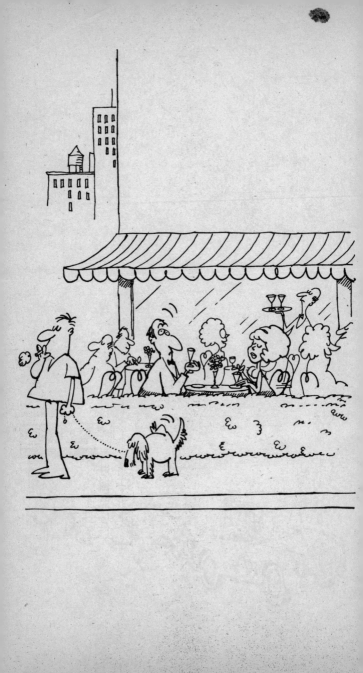

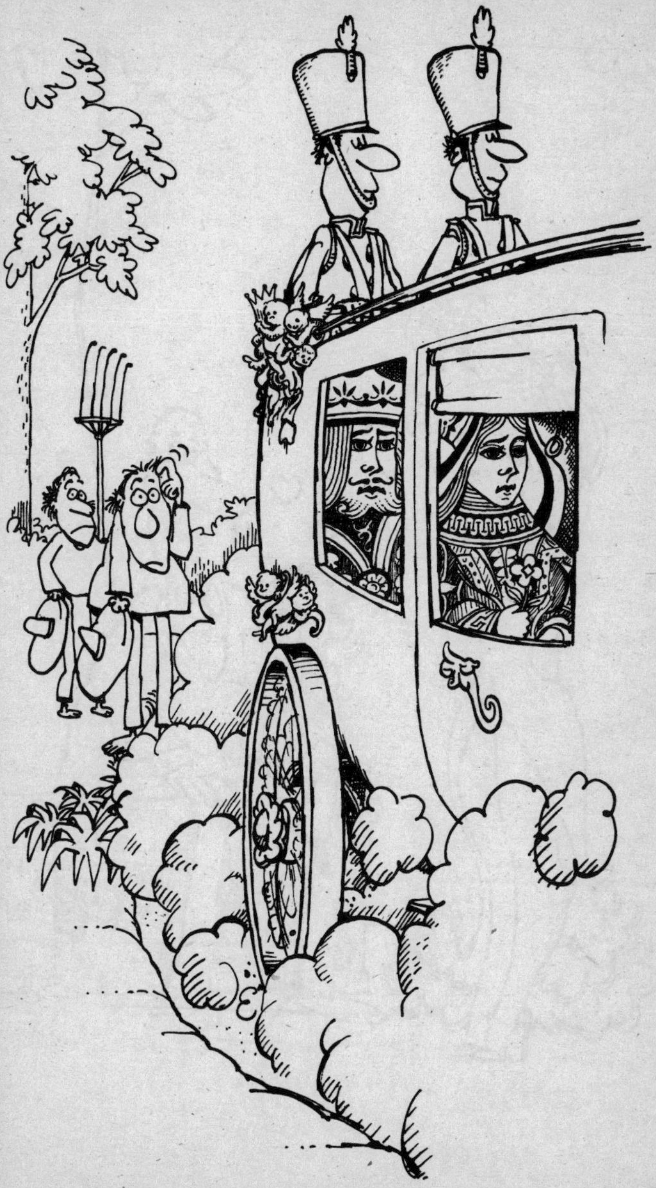

1

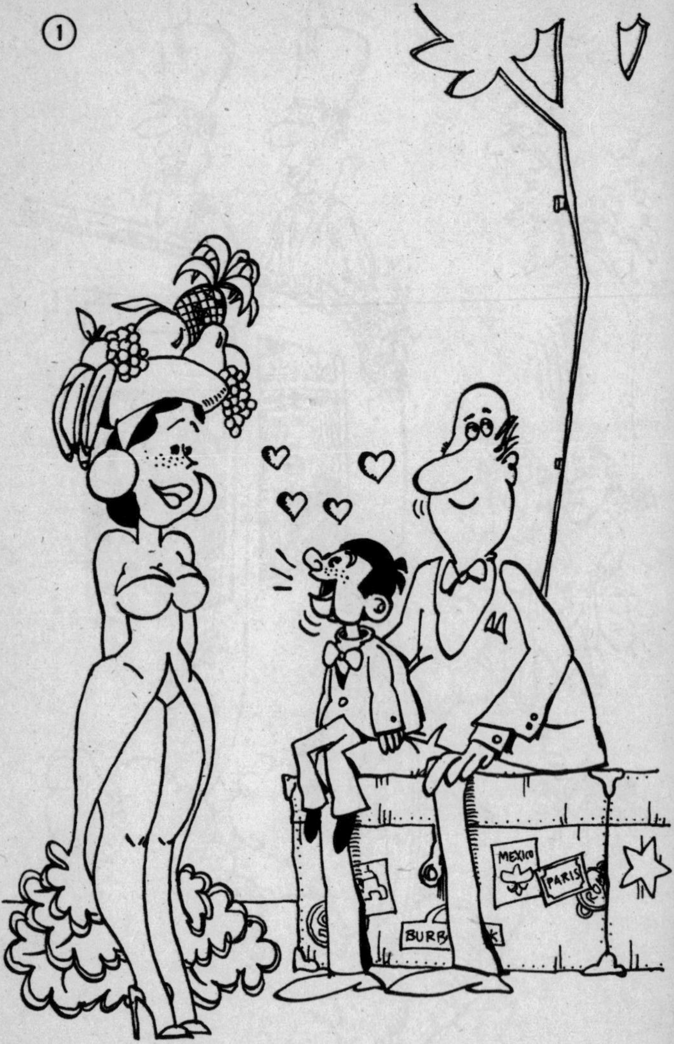
MEXICO
PARIS

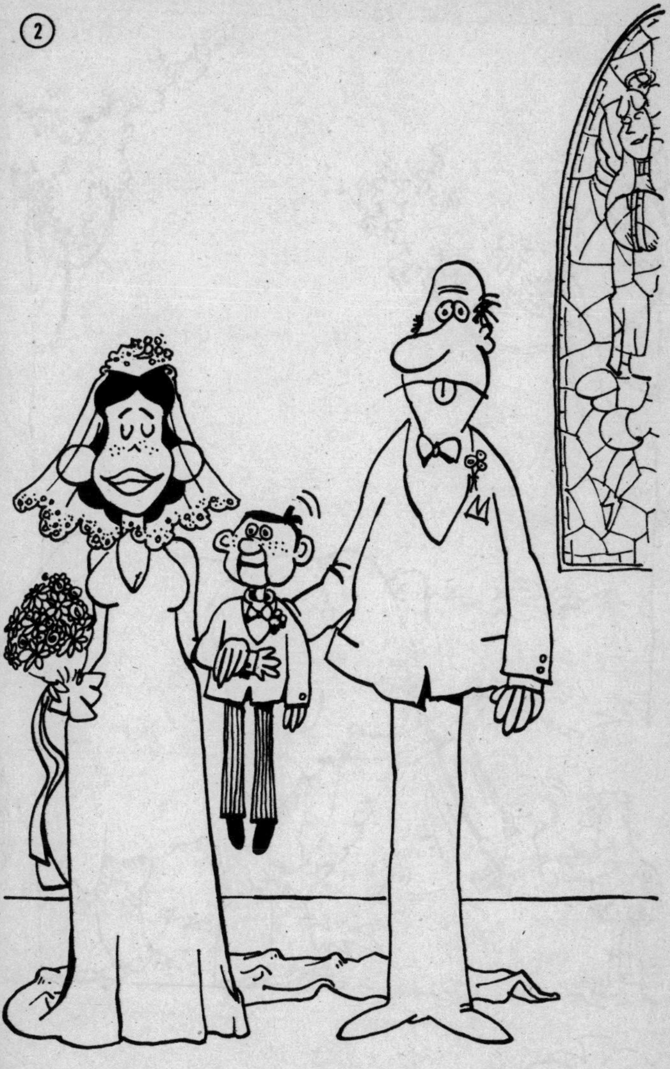

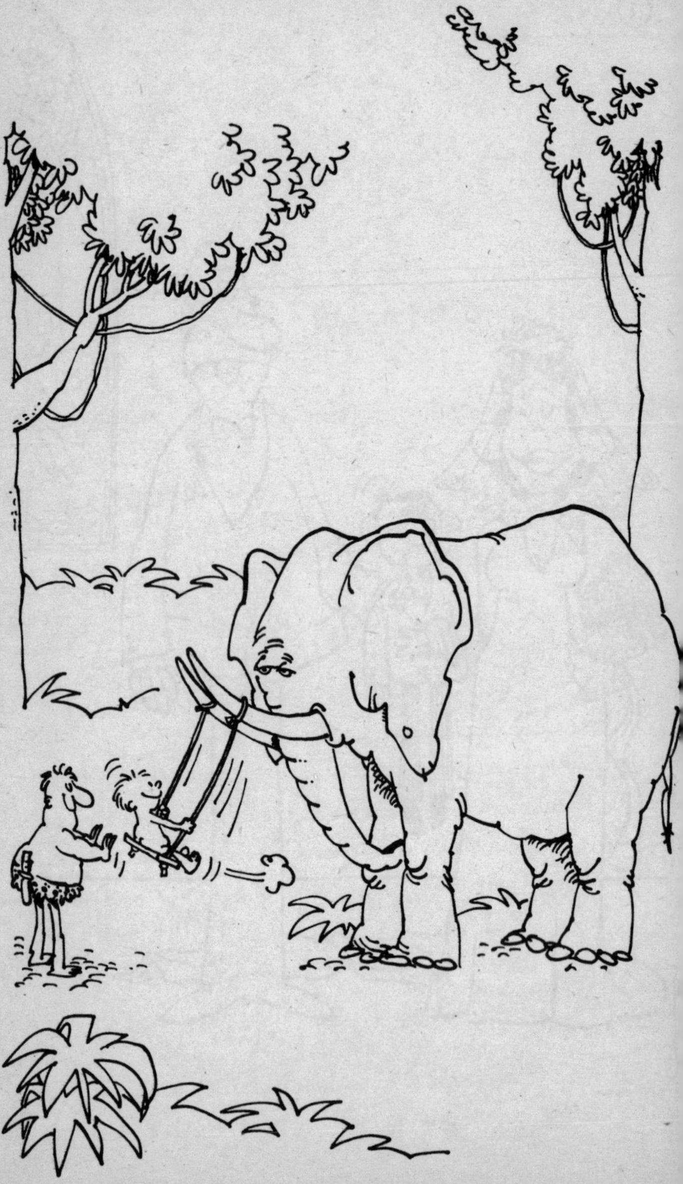

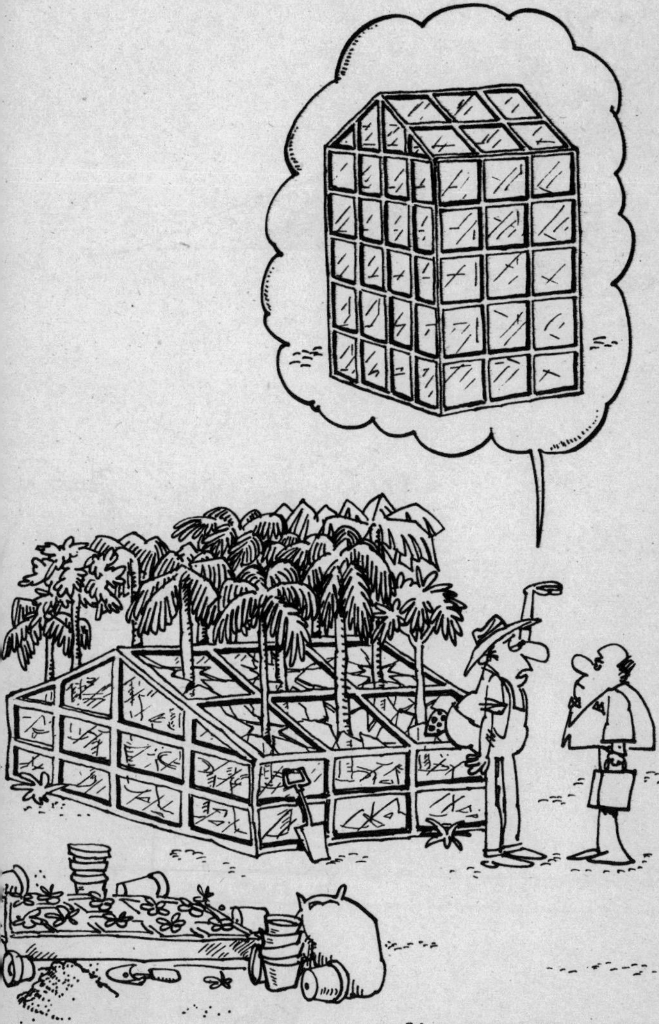

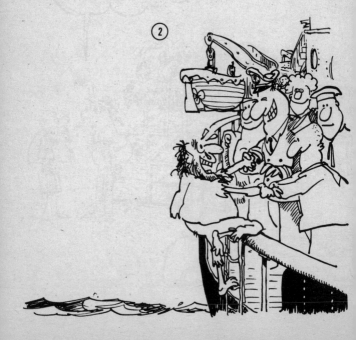

3

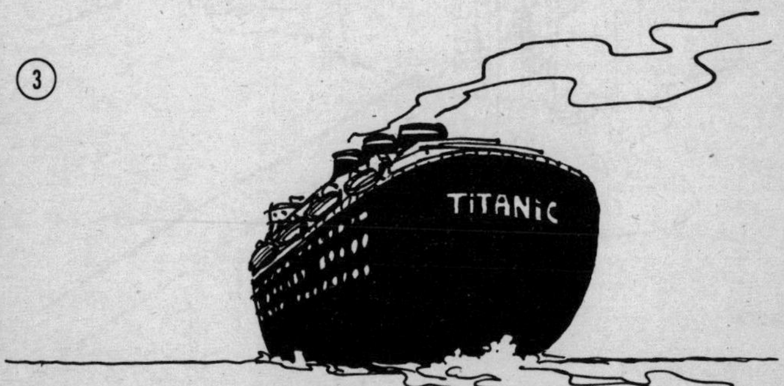
TITANIC

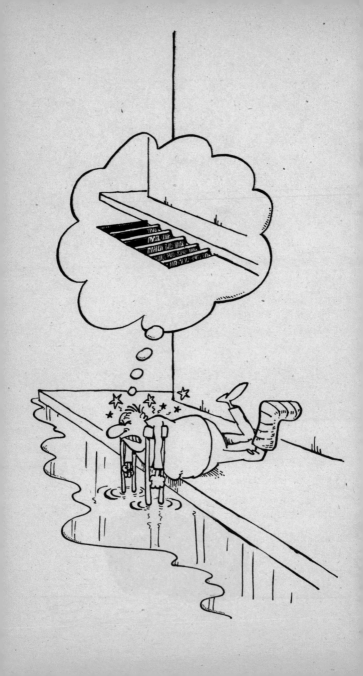

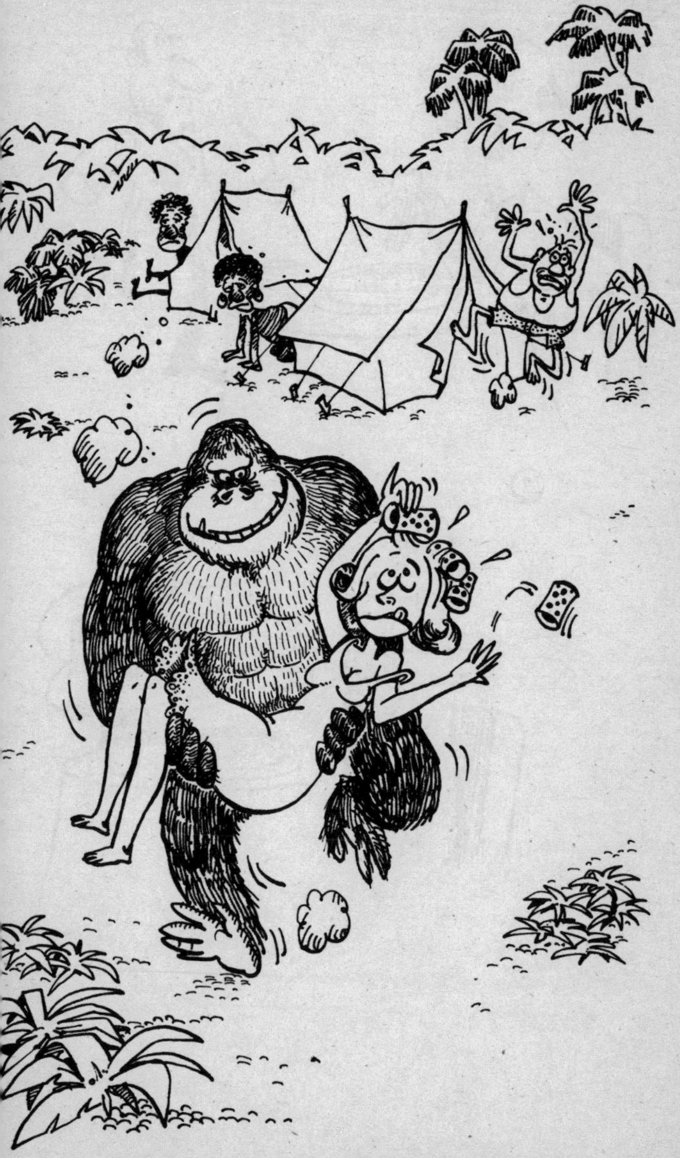

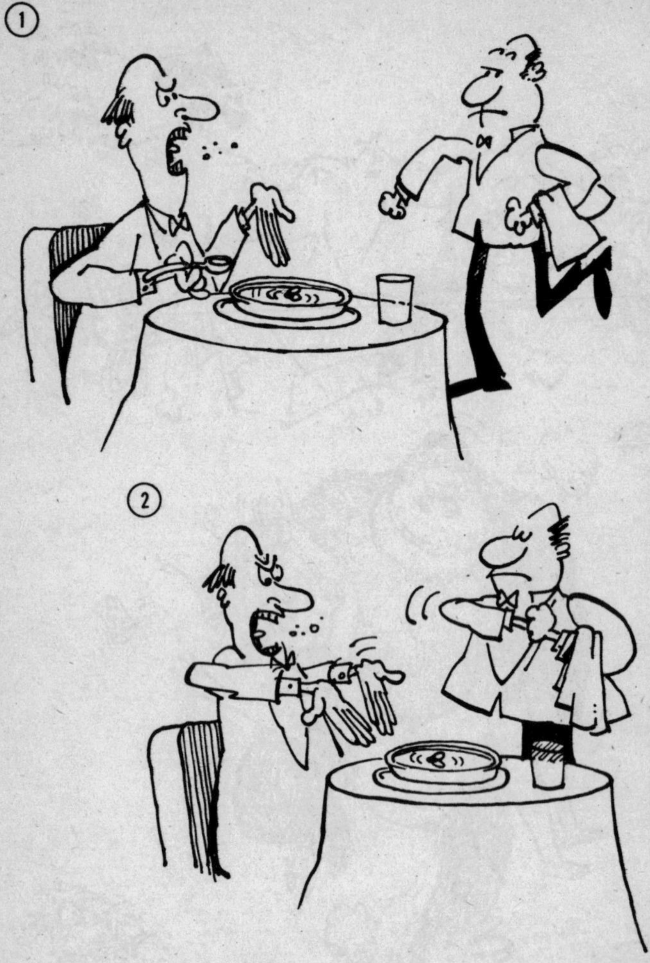
1
2

3

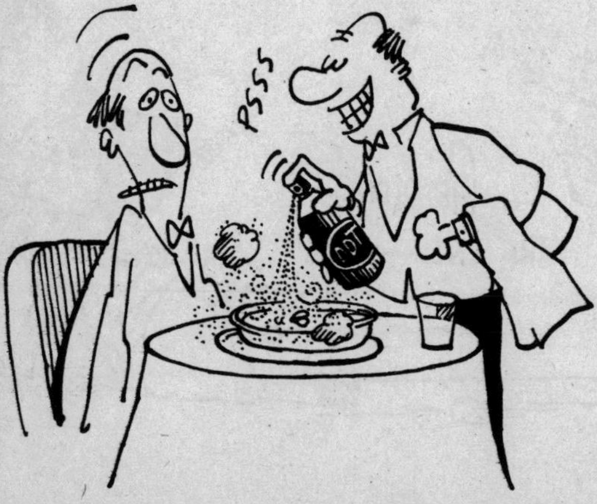
PSSS
DDT

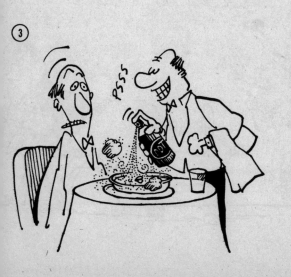

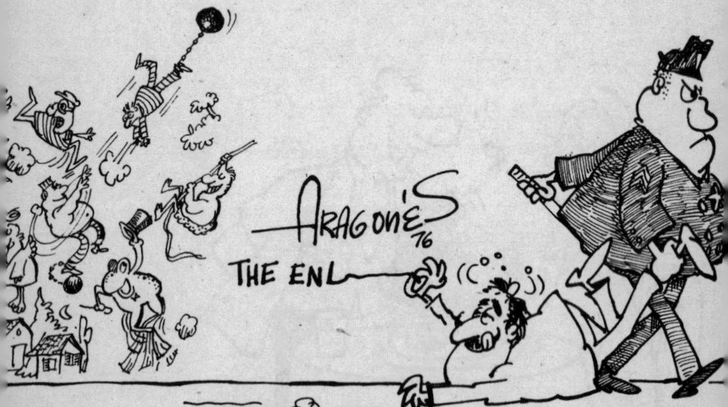
ARAGONÉS 76
THE ENL